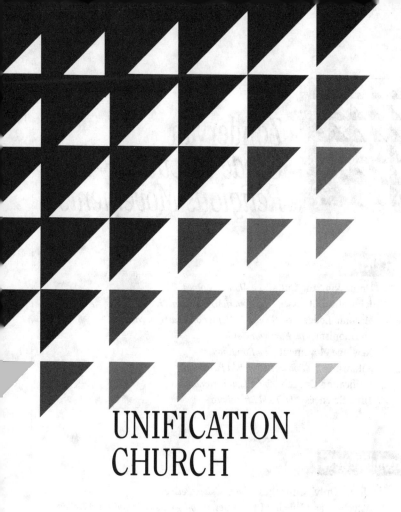

UNIFICATION
CHURCH

Zondervan
Guide to Cults &
Religious Movements

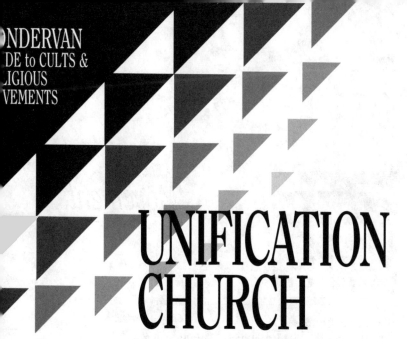

UNIFICATION CHURCH

J. ISAMU YAMAMOTO
Author

Alan W. Gomes
Series Editor

ZondervanPublishingHouse
Grand Rapids, Michigan

A Division of HarperCollinsPublishers

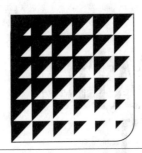

Unification Church
Copyright © 1995 by J. Isamu Yamamoto

Requests for information should be addressed to:
　Zondervan Publishing House
　Grand Rapids, Michigan 49530

Library of Congress Cataloging-in-Publication Data

Yamamoto, J. Isamu.
　Unification Church / J. Isamu Yamamoto.
　　　p.　cm. — (Zondervan guide to cults and religious movements)
　Includes bibliographical references.
　ISBN 0-310-70381-6 (pbk.)
　1. Unification Church—Controversial literature.　I. Title.
　II. Series.
　BX9750.S44Y36　　1995
　289.9'6—dc20　　　　　　　　　　　　　　　　　94-33439
　　　　　　　　　　　　　　　　　　　　　　　　　　　　CIP

Edited by Patti Picardi
Interior design by Art Jacobs

Printed in the United States of America

95 96 97 98 99 00 / ❖ DP / 10 9 8 7 6 5 4 3 2 1

Contents

How to Use This Book

The *Zondervan Guide to Cults and Religious Movements* comprises sixteen volumes, treating many of the most important groups and belief systems confronting the Christian church today. This series distills the most important facts about each and presents a well-reasoned, cogent Christian response. The authors in this series are highly qualified, well-respected professional Christian apologists with considerable expertise on their topics.

For ease of use we have sought to maintain the same "look and feel" for all the books. We designed the structure and layout to help you find the information you need as quickly as possible.

All the volumes are written in outline form. This allows us to pack substantial content into a short book. The major divisions are basically the same from book to book. Each book contains an introduction to the cult, movement, or belief system. The introduction gives a brief history of the group, its organizational structure, and vital statistics such as membership. The theology section is arranged by doctrinal topic, such as God, Christ, sin, and salvation. The movement's position on each topic is set forth objectively, primarily from its own official writings. The group's teachings are then refuted point by point, followed by an affirmative presentation of what the Bible says about the doctrine. Following the theology section is a discussion of witnessing tips. While each witnessing encounter must be handled individually and sensitively, this section provides some helpful general guidelines, including both dos and don'ts. The books also have an annotated bibliography, listing works by the groups themselves as well as books written by Christians in response. Each book concludes with a parallel comparison chart. Arranged topically, the chart juxtaposes direct quotations from the cultic literature in the left column with the biblical refutation on the right.

One potential problem with a detailed outline is that it is easy to lose one's place in the overall structure. To overcome this problem we have provided graphical "signposts" at the top of the odd-numbered pages. Functioning like a "you are here" map in a shopping mall, these graphics show your place in the outline, including the sections that come before and after your current position. In the theology section we have also used "icons" in the margins to make clear at a glance whether the material is being presented from the cultic or Christian viewpoint. For example, in the Mormonism volume those portions of the outline presenting the Mormon position are indicated with a picture of the angel Moroni in the margin. The biblical view is shown by a drawing of a Bible.

We hope you will find these books useful as you seek "to give an answer to everyone who asks you to give the reason for the hope that you have" (1 Peter 3:15).

—Alan W. Gomes, Ph.D.
Series Editor

 # Part I:
Introduction

I.Historical Background[1]

A. Sun Myung Moon: Youth Through Early Adulthood

1. Sun Myung Moon was born on January 6, 1920, in the village of Kwangju Sangsa Ri in northwestern Korea.

2. According to Moon, as a young "Christian" he had a dramatic spiritual experience while he was deep in prayer on a Korean mountainside.

   a. This vision occurred on Easter morning in 1936 when he was sixteen.

   b. He says that Jesus appeared to him and asked him to complete the mission he had begun 2000 years ago.

   c. When he realized that he was the only one who could save the world, he accepted the call to deliver all humanity from Satan's domain.

3. Moon claims that he spent the following nine years in spiritual warfare with Satan, in which Satan tried to get Moon to either sin (and thus be unworthy to be the Messiah) or be convinced that he could not accomplish all that the Messiah must do to redeem humanity. Finally, he defeated Satan, thus fulfilling the initial demands of being the Messiah.

4. In 1946, Moon studied under Paik Moon Kim. Much of what he learned in Kim's pseudo-Christian monastery became the framework for his own theological teachings.

5. In that same year, the North Korean police arrested Moon.

   a. Moon insists that they tortured him because of his faith.

   b. He likened his suffering at the hands of the communists to the sufferings of Christ.

---

[1]The biography of Sun Myung Moon and the history of the Unification Church are taken from the following sources, which were published by the Unification Church or are materials sympathetic to this movement and have its approval: Mose Durst, *To Bigotry, No Sanction: Reverend Sun Myung Moon and the Unification Church* (Chicago: Regnery Gateway, 1984); Won Pil Kim, "Father's Early Ministry in Pusan," *Today's World* (May 1982); Carlton Sherwood, *Inquisition: The Persecution and Prosecution of the Reverend Sun Myung Moon* (Washington, D.C.: Regnery Gateway, 1991); Frederick Sontag, *Sun Myung Moon and the Unification Church* (Nashville: Abingdon, 1977); and the leaflet "Sun Myung Moon, A Biography" (Berkeley: Unification Church, n.d.). Since I am critical of Moon's teachings, I have used these sources to provide a fair representation of him and his movement.

6. In 1948, Moon was arrested a second time and sentenced to five years of hard labor at Hung Nam, North Korea.

   a. The Korean War interrupted his prison term.

   b. During the fighting between the communists and the United Nations' forces, Moon escaped and fled to South Korea.

B. *Moon's Activities as Church Founder*

1. Moon settled in Pusan, South Korea.

   a. There he formed a small following during the early 1950s.

   b. These people were devoted both to Moon and to his religious ideas.

   c. They called him "Reverend" because they viewed him as their pastor and because of his religious training at Kim's monastery.

2. In 1954, he officially established his new church.

   a. It is called Tong-il-Kyo in Korean.

   b. Its English name is the Holy Spirit Association for the Unification of World Christianity.

   c. It is better known in the West as the Unification Church (it is also known as the Unified Family).

3. In that same year, Moon's first wife left him.

   a. According to leaders in the Unification Church, she later realized that she was wrong to have divorced him.

   b. She has since become a devoted member of his church.

4. In 1957, he published the first edition of the *Divine Principle*, which details the basic theology of his teachings and of the Unification Church (see III.B.3. below).

5. In 1960, he married Hak Ja Han.

   a. In the Unification Church their wedding is known as "the Marriage of the Lamb," taken from Revelation 21:9.

   b. She has since bore him thirteen children.

C. *Moon's Activities as Church Leader*

1. During the late fifties, membership in the Unification Church grew at a steady rate while spreading throughout South Korea.

2. His movement soon extended to Japan, where Moon has enjoyed his second largest following.

3. In 1959, Moon sent his first missionary, Young Oon Kim, to the United States to establish churches in North America.

4. Moon visited the United States in the sixties.

5. However, it was not until his seven-city "Day of Hope" tour, from late 1971 to early 1972, that his movement began to attract large numbers of Westerners.

6. The U.S. news media became fascinated with Moon for two reasons:

    a. Moon was one of the few people to publicly support Richard Nixon during the winter of 1973–74, when the Nixon Administration was entering its stormiest period of the Watergate scandal.

      (1) On November 30, 1973, Moon took time from his second "Day of Hope" tour to issue a statement, which was printed in twenty-one major newspapers across the United States.

      (2) Essentially, Moon said that only God should remove Nixon from the presidency since God had chosen Nixon to be president.

      (3) When Nixon invited Moon to the White House, the press quickly became fascinated with this Korean religious leader.

    b. As an integral element in the life of his church, Moon had been conducting mass marriages, in which he usually selected who should marry whom. (Unificationists view marriage as a holy sacrament like communion and baptism.)

      (1) In February 1975, Moon married eighteen hundred couples in Seoul, Korea, from twenty-five countries, including seventy couples from the United States.

      (2) It was the largest single ceremony thus far in the Unification Church, and it further drew him into the spotlight of the Western press.

D. Moon as a Controversial Figure

  1. Controversy over Recruiting

    a. Moon became a much more controversial figure when the recruiting practices of the Unification Church became publicly known.

    b. Critics of Moon claimed that leaders of his church had brainwashed many of his followers.[2]

  2. Controversy over Finances

    a. The rapid growth of his financial empire in North America became a public issue.

    b. Moon's church purchased property and his followers established industries in the United States at an alarming rate.

---

[2]Carroll Stoner and Jo Anne Parke, *All God's Children: The Cult Experience—Salvation or Slavery?* (Radnor, Penn.: Chilton Book Co., 1977), 154–55; Janice Harayda, "I Was a Robot for Sun Myung Moon," *Glamour* (April 1976); Gerald Kemp, "Parents Fight 'Brainwashing' by Bizarre Sect," *London Daily Telegraph* (May 3, 1976); Stan Whitley, "Moon Follower Talks of Brainwashing Attempts," *Great Bend Tribune* (October 14, 1975). Note that I myself do not believe people in the Unification Church are "brainwashed." See Part III, "Witnessing Tips," II.A.2.a. See also the following sources that are critical of the brainwashing perspective: Eileen Barker, *The Making of a Moonie: Choice or Brainwashing?* (New York: Basil Blackwell, 1984); David G. Bromley and Anson D. Shupe, Jr., *"Moonies" in America: Cult, Church, and Crusade* (Beverly Hills: Sage Publications, 1979); and Thomas Robbins and Dick Anthony, "New Religions, Families and Brainwashing," in Robbins and Anthony, eds. *In Gods We Trust* (New Brunswick, N.J.: Transaction Books, 1981).

    c. Moon and his family took up permanent residence in New York City, where they live in affluence.

  3. Controversy over Messianic Claims

    a. What alarmed Jews and Christians the most was, and still is, Moon's implication, and some of his followers' proclamation, that he is the Messiah.

    b. Especially disturbing to Christians in particular is his teaching that Jesus did not fulfill his mission, and therefore another messiah must complete Christ's earthly ministry.

E. *Moon's Legal Entanglements—Major Cases Involving the Unification Church*

  1. Katz v. Superior Court (1977)

    a. In San Francisco parents filed and won conservatorship of their adult children, who were members of the Unification Church.

    b. The California Court of Appeals reversed Judge Vavuris's judgment, ruling that they were mentally competent.

  2. Molko and Leal v. Holy Spirit Association (1986)

    a. David Molko and Tracy Leal brought a suit against the Unification Church.

      (1) Molko and Leal were former members of the Unification Church.

      (2) They charged that the Unification Church had brainwashed them.

    b. The lower courts dismissed the case.

    c. However, the California Supreme Court reversed the lower courts.

      (1) In October 1988, the court ruled that this suit could be brought to trial.

      (2) In fact, the justices said that the Unification Church could be liable for fraud, infliction of emotional distress, and restitution.

    d. This ruling has been appealed to the Supreme Court, which still has not acted on it.

F. *Moon's Legal Entanglements—A Major Case Involving Himself*[3]

  1. The Charges

    a. On October 22, 1981, Moon pleaded not guilty to a set of indictments ranging from fraud to tax evasion.

    b. Most of these charges centered on the interest that had accumulated in Moon's account in a Chase Manhattan Bank but had not been reported to the Internal Revenue Service during the early seventies.

---

[3]See John T. Biermans, *The Odyssey of New Religions Today: A Case of the Unification Church* (Lewiston, N.Y.: Edwin Mellen, 1988); John McClaughry, "The Uneasy Case against Reverend Moon," *National Review* (December 23, 1982); and Sherwood, *Inquisition*. Sherwood's book provides an exhaustive, though favorably biased, account of the proceedings, drawing from court transcripts and interviews with the participants in the case against Moon. Note that Biermans and McClaughry are also favorably biased toward Moon.

(1) The Justice Department claimed that $1.5 million had been deposited into Moon's account, which he used for himself. Therefore, he should have reported the interest earned on those funds and paid the proper taxes.

(2) Moon's attorney contended that the funds belonged to the Unification Church and were used for church-related purposes. Since Moon was trustee of church funds, it was not uncommon to have church funds in a bank account in his name.

2. The Verdict

a. On May 18, 1982, a New York jury found Moon guilty of evading several thousand dollars in income taxes.

b. Moon was sentenced to eighteen months in jail and fined $25,000, plus the costs of prosecution.

c. He served thirteen months, receiving five months off for good behavior. On August 20, 1985, he was released from the federal prison in Danbury, Connecticut.

d. Friends of Moon note that Moon "stood trial, [was] convicted, sentenced, and then jailed on a voluntary basis . . . Moon . . . could have simply boarded a plane and left the U.S. at anytime."[4]

3. Moon as "Martyr"

a. The stigma of being a convicted felon did not tarnish Moon's image in the eyes of his followers and sympathizers.

b. In fact, they regard him as a martyr, who has suffered unjustly, just as he had at the hands of the communists, who had imprisoned him.

c. Moon's followers compare the persecution of their "Master" with the persecution of Christ.

d. In addition, some say that "Because of his willingness to go this course voluntarily, without complaint, he is now seen as a leading champion and spokesman for religious freedom."[5]

II. The Unification Church

A. *Structure*

1. Sun Myung Moon officially started the Unification Church in Korea in 1954.

2. Since then his church has been established in countries throughout the world.

3. Unification missionaries currently have entered formerly communist nations in Europe.

---

[4]Sherwood, 416.
[5]Biermans, 225.

4. The number of members in the Unification Church is far greater in Korea and Japan than anywhere else.

5. Nevertheless, Moon's church in the United States still plays a significant role in Moon's plans to expand his church and spread his teachings. Moon believes it is through the United States that he can best exert his influence globally, since the United States is the world's leading economic, political, and military nation.

6. The Eastern and Western branches have at times clashed over bureaucratic issues, particularly the Unification leaders in Korea and the United States, with the Korean church usually winning out.

7. The Unification Church is divided into nations, regions (districts), and individual churches, and governed accordingly.

B. Recruitment

1. During the seventies, the Unification Church was widely condemned for its recruiting practices.

   a. Stories of "brainwashed Moonies" headlined newspapers and periodicals in the West during this time.[6]

   b. There were also a number of articles on "kidnapping" and "deprogramming."[7]

2. Unification officials admit that in some cases, overzealous district leaders applied too much pressure on people to join and remain within the group. They disagree, however, with the accusation that they brainwash their followers.

   a. Unification officials further state that they have since corrected these practices in which people both inside and outside the Unification Church were not given truthful information about Moon and his movement.

   b. Some critics of the Unification Church, however, claim that these abuses were systematically directed from the top, faithfully carried out among all branches of the church, and are still applied today—though much more subtly.

      (1) Historian Ruth Tucker notes that "The recruitment strategy of the Unification Church was widely criticized for utilizing tactics that were sometimes compared to brainwashing techniques."[8]

---

[6]See footnotes 1 and 2.

[7]Dean M. Kelley, "Deprogramming and Religious Liberty," *The Civil Liberties Review* (July/August 1977); John Knoble, "Moonie, Deprogrammer Trade Swipes," *New Haven Register* (November 21, 1976); W. F. Willoughby, "A Futile Try to Deprogram a Believer," *Washington Star* (September 3, 1975); Mel Ziegler, "The Man Who 'Deprograms' Moonies," *San Francisco Chronicle* (December 12, 1975).

[8]Ruth A. Tucker, *Another Gospel: Alternative Religions and the New Age Movement* (Grand Rapids: Zondervan, 1989), 257.

(2) Walter Martin said that the Unification Church is "characterized by what appears to be obvious, widespread, and forceful psychological pressure on members to conform and remain loyal to the group at all costs."[9]

c. Other authorities on the Unification Church argue that these abuses were not widespread.

(1) Sociologists David Bromley and Anson Shupe claim that these psychological abuses occurred mainly in the Oakland, California branch, which was led by Mose Durst.[10]

(2) Professor Eileen Barker at the London School of Economics and Political Science affirms Bromley and Shupe's view: "A third [of the Unification Church members surveyed] did not realize that they were in Moon's Unification Church until they had heard several lectures or, in some (mainly California) cases, until they had actually joined the movement."[11]

d. It seems reasonable to conclude that in the seventies and eighties systematic and more serious abuses took place in the Unification Church, especially at the Oakland branch. Since that time, at least the major abuses do not appear to be an issue.

3. The following are the major complaints that have emerged against the recruiting practices of the Unification Church.

a. "Heavenly Deception"

(1) The term "heavenly deception" emerged from the teaching that lying is good if it is for the purpose of saving that person, or if it advances "the kingdom of God" (that is, Moon's church). In other words, Unificationists lied about their group and Moon's teachings to potential converts.

(2) Chris Elkins, from his experiences in the Unification Church, defines heavenly deception as "the policy of using falsehood to achieve, supposedly, goodness. . . . Heavenly deception is a thread that extends far into the fabric of the Unification Church."[12]

(3) I personally have observed Unificationists practice heavenly deception on numerous occasions. For example, I have encountered Unificationists in wheelchairs soliciting funds for social programs that did not exist, and when I asked them why they pretended to be disabled as they walked to their van, they used their concept of heavenly deception to defend their actions.

---

[9]Walter Martin, *The Kingdom of the Cults*, rev. and exp. ed. (Minneapolis: Bethany House, 1985), 338.

[10]Bromley and Shupe, 36–37.

[11]Barker, 177.

[12]Chris Elkins, *Heavenly Deception* (Wheaton, Ill.: Tyndale House, 1980), 14.

b. Limiting Outside Contact

(1) The Unification Church secluded its members from anyone outside the movement.

(2) Unification leaders taught members that anyone outside their church is an instrument of Satan.

(3) These outsiders included family and friends.

(4) For example, in Christopher Edwards' account, he said prior to his leaving the Unification Church, "It was just as the Family said. Satan lurked in my parents, tempting me with their fallen love."[13]

(5) I have found this belief to be true with some Unificationists but not all.

c. Slave Labor Conditions

(1) Members were forced to work long hours studying the teachings of the church, raising money for the church, or enlisting new members into the church.

(2) Little sleep and poor diet may have contributed to their loyalty to Moon. Journalists Carroll Stoner and Jo Anne Parke note that Moon's "young followers live severe lives of self-denial."[14]

(3) It would be an overstatement, however, to characterize members' austere lifetyle as slave labor conditions, particularly when some legitimate Christian communities also lead austere lives as a reflection of their devotion to Christ.[15]

d. Arranged Marriages

(1) The Unification Church—primarily Moon—selected who was to marry whom within his church. (In many cases they married total strangers or someone they barely knew.)

(2) Asian cultural factors should be taken into account here.

(3) Historian Ruth Tucker notes: "The seemingly random pairing of couples by Moon is not as peculiar to the Asian observer, who may be used to arranged marriages, as to the Westerner who is often dismayed by the practice."[16]

e. Moon's Authoritarianism

(1) Unification leaders teach members that Moon is the most important authority figure in their lives—that their only purpose is to please "Father" (Moon).

---

[13]Christopher Edwards, *Crazy for God: The Nightmare of Cult Life* (Englewood Cliffs, N.J.: Prentice Hall, 1979), 212.

[14]Stoner and Parke, 196.

[15]Recent Christian examples include the Berkeley Christian Coalition in Berkeley, California, and Jesus People USA in Chicago, Illinois.

[16]Tucker, 256.

(2) Sociologist Ronald Enroth believes Moon is "filled with delusions of messianic grandeur."[17]

(3) Enroth records a pledge that the Unificationists recite: "I will fulfill our Father's [Moon's] will, and the responsibility given me. I will become a dutiful son and a child of goodness to attend to our Father [Moon] forever."[18]

(4) Enroth is correct when he concludes that Moon believes he is the Messiah and that his authority in the Unification Church is absolute.

C. Finances

The financial empire of Moon and his church is noteworthy because it is used primarily to finance the spread of his doctrines.

1. Size of Moon's Financial Empire

   a. Although there is no way to determine the exact figure, even the Unification Church admits that individual members have collected tens of millions of dollars in the United States alone in the past twenty years.[19]

   b. In North America, either Moon's church or members have acquired valuable property and numerous small businesses. (The New Yorker hotel and *The Washington Times* newspaper are two good examples.)

   c. Despite the visible presence of Moon's financial empire in the North America, church operations and other activities related to Moon's religious, social, and political programs in the West have been an economic burden to the Unification Church.

      (1) It has been wrongly speculated that American and Canadian dollars are sent to Korea.

      (2) The Korean and Japanese branches of the church are actually bankrolling their sister churches in the West.[20]

2. Deceptiveness in Fundraising

   a. Critics argue that many members have told prospective givers that their donations would be used for social programs that did not exist, as well as falsifying who they themselves were. Again, church officials have admitted that these abuses occurred, but that they

---

[17]Ronald Enroth, *Youth, Brainwashing and the Extremist Cults* (Grand Rapids: Zondervan, 1977), 110.

[18]Enroth, 116.

[19]In 1979, Neil Salonen, then president of the Unification Church in the United States, related to me that Unificationists in the U.S. had collected about $6,000,000 during the previous year. *Time* magazine reported that the Unification Church had raised about $10,000,000 a year in the early seventies; *see*, "The Darker Side of Sun Myung Moon," *Time* (June 14, 1976), 50. According to Stoner and Parke (195), such fundraising in 1973 probably reaped more than $18,000,000.

[20]Again, Neil Salonen conveyed this information to me.

went against the instructions of the church and have been corrected.[21]

b. For example, Mose Durst, who directed the Oakland branch of the Unification Church during this controversial time, and who later became president of the Unification Church in the United States, admits: "If the anti-religious movement and the criminal activities directed against the Unification Church have served some good, it has allowed us to think more honestly and clearly about the mistakes I and others have made in our zeal to build the Kingdom of God on earth. There have been many mistakes, but none of them malicious, devious, illegal, or intended to defraud as our detractors charge. Rather, our mistakes are those made in youthful zeal and out of ignorance."[22]

D. Public Relations

1. Overcoming Negative Perceptions

   a. The campaign of Moon and the Unification Church to erase the terrible image that most Americans have of him and his church has been somewhat successful.

   b. Indeed, "the Unification Church has spent millions of dollars to polish its tarnished image."[23]

   c. Although many people still regard Moon's church as a cult, an expensive and considerable effort to improve relations with political, social, and religious organizations has substantially silenced the alarm that pervaded the American public in the seventies.

   d. In addition, "in its effort to present itself as just another persecuted minority religion, the Unification Church has succeeded in gaining the sympathy of many prominent intellectuals."[24]

   e. Also, the media simply lost interest in Moon.

2. Building Bridges to the Politically Conservative

   a. A central element in Moon's theology is that communism is Satan's tool.

   b. Since Moon has invested a great deal of energy and money to combat communism, he has been able to build bridges with some politically conservative groups. He has also established political organizations and annual conferences that have enlisted the cooperation and participation of some political leaders from the right (see III.C. below).

---

[21]Barker, 101.

[22]Durst, 155. Of course, one might question whether Durst's statement is itself a specimen of "heavenly deception," coming as it does from a Unification Church leader. Based on independent observations, it appears that this statement is generally true.

[23]Stoner and Parke, 5.

[24]Tucker, 265.

3. Racial Unity

   a. Moon's teaching also stresses the unity of the races.

   b. Moon has sponsored seminars to improve race relations, drawing upon the cooperation of social groups who are interested in the same goals, such as the NAACP.

4. Ecumenical Outreach

   a. Improving its relationships with other religious organizations has been a primary goal of the Unification Church.

   b. To accomplish this, Moon has invited church leaders to exotic locations around the world to discuss theology and find areas of common ground.

   c. Members of the Unification Church have made significant efforts to develop friendly relationships with local pastors.

   d. Articulate leaders from the Unification Church have persuaded Christian leaders to join with their church in actively resisting government actions that seemingly threaten all religious groups.

III. Vital Statistics

A. *Membership Figures*

1. Difficulty of Assessing Accurate Membership Figures

   a. The Unification Church is extremely reluctant to release statistical information about itself, particularly about membership figures.

   b. The public relations department of the church says unscrupulous opponents gather such data deceptively and then distort figures to create negative impressions of Moon and his church; that is, they make Moon's movement appear to be a threat to American society.

   c. Consequently, as a matter of policy, they distribute such information only after inquirers have met very restrictive guidelines.

   d. Numerous sources have cited a wide range of figures that further muddle the problem.

   e. Nevertheless, a reasonable calculation can be formulated.

2. Estimated Membership

   a. Membership in the Unification Church worldwide is probably somewhere between one and two million.

      (1) Most Unificationists are either Korean or Japanese.

      (2) The number of North American Unificationists is likely between ten and thirty thousand.

   b. Consider also the many people who have strong ties either to the Unification Church or to one of Moon's other organizations, but who are not technically members. Since Moon has established many groups, the number of full-time followers and part-time supporters probably sets the number at the higher ranges.

B. *Literature Distribution*

1. Difficulty of Assessing Accurate Publication Figures

    a. It is difficult to determine the volume of literature that the Unification Church distributes.

    b. Most of its affiliate organizations publish a newsletter, journal, or some other type of literature.

    c. They publish materials not only for its members, but also for non-members who are interested in a specific subject matter, such as anticommunism.

2. Estimated Publication Statistics

    a. Moon's operations print millions of pieces of literature annually.

    b. Some discuss theology, others promote political views, and still others address social issues.

3. The *Divine Principle*

    a. Written by Moon, this book is the primary source for Unification Church doctrine.

    b. The Unification Church has published the *Divine Principle* in different languages and several editions.

    c. It is not sold publicly.

    d. Although there are a vast number of copies of this book, it is still difficult to obtain, since the Unification Church tries to keep copies within its membership.

    e. How many copies do exist in all its various forms is not known to the general public.

C. *Related Groups and Organizations*

1. The Unification Theological Seminary

    a. The Unification Church has a seminary in Barrytown, New York called The Unification Theological Seminary.

    b. It is used as a theological training center, where members are prepared to be leaders and theologians in the church.

    c. Since many people regard Moon as a cult leader, there is a false impression that this seminary is academically weak.

    d. Moon's seminary, however, has not only attracted a respectable faculty (many of whom are not members of his church), but it also has graduated many students (who are members of his church) who have been accepted into doctoral programs at institutions such as Harvard and Yale.

2. The One World Crusade (OWC)

    a. OWC is the evangelistic arm of the Unification Church.

    b. OWC was far more prominent in Moon's efforts to attract Westerners in the seventies.

    c. OWC sponsored Moon's earlier tours (such as the "Day of Hope" tours) and spawned several other groups (like the *International Cultural Foundation*) that target specific types of people, such as in the areas of cultural exchange and sporting activities.

3. The Collegiate Association for the Research of Principles (CARP)

    a. CARP has been active on college campuses for decades as an organization that promotes conservative social and political values.

    b. At times CARP has been very subtle about its association with the Unification Church, however, the link between the two has always been strong, since the purpose of both is to spread Moon's teachings.

4. World Freedom Institute (WFI)

    a. The most notable political organization founded by Moon is the WFI.

    b. Formerly known as the Freedom Leadership Foundation, the WFI promotes various groups against communism.

    c. It distributes a weekly newspaper called *The Rising Tide,* which reports on communist and leftist activities.

    d. Although communism has dissolved in many places around the world, posing less of a threat to the West, North Korea still exists as a powerful communist state. Thus, Moon's campaign against communism has not slackened.

5. New Ecumenical Research Association

    a. This organization sponsors professional conferences where evangelicals, scientists, lawyers, and journalists are invited to speak.

    b. The conferences are intended to attract scholars and leaders in these fields to promote unity within their fields and to foster legitimacy for Moon and his church in the eyes of the participants.

6. International Religious Foundation

    a. This organization sponsors interfaith dialogues.

    b. It held the First Assembly of the World's Religions in New Jersey in 1985.

7. Other Related Groups

    a. The list of related groups is too long to describe.

    b. Many serve their purpose and are disbanded while others are formed for new tasks.

    c. All of them, in one way or another, seek to promote Moon's conception of the kingdom of God on earth.

Part II: Theology

I. Divine Revelation

A. *The Unification Church's Position on Divine Revelation Briefly Stated*

1. God has revealed his truth to Sun Myung Moon.

2. God's revelations to Sun Myung Moon are disclosed in the *Divine Principle*.

3. The *Divine Principle* contains the basic tenets and doctrines of the Unification Church.

4. The *Divine Principle* is the third testament of the Bible and is as authoritative as the Old and New Testaments.

B. *Arguments Used by the Unification Church to Support Its Position on Divine Revelation*

1. Human history is divided into three dispensations.

   a. The Law of Moses governed the Old Testament age.

   b. The teachings of Christ governed the New Testament age.

   c. The doctrines of the *Divine Principle* currently govern the Completed Testament age (henceforth from the time Moon revealed his teachings).

2. The revelations that God has revealed to Moon take precedence over the Old and New Testaments.

   a. In each age God dispenses only as much truth as people can grasp.

      (1) In the Old Testament age people could grasp only what God conveyed through Moses and the prophets.

      (2) In the New Testament age people could understand the teachings of the Old Testament, Jesus, and the apostles.

      (3) Presently, people have matured to a spiritual level where God can reveal all truth (given through Moon).

   b. The *Divine Principle* states that God has sent Moon to resolve the fundamental questions of life and the universe.[25]

---

[25]*Divine Principle*, 2d ed. (Washington, D.C.: HSA-UWC, 1973), 16. The *Divine Principle* is the authoritative document of the Unification Church. Although other books provide spiritual guidance to Unificationists, the *Divine Principle* is the only book that nearly all Unificationists accept.

c. Young Oon Kim, the leading theologian of the Unification Church, puts it this way: "We believe that God revealed to Reverend Moon the fundamental core of his teaching."[26]

d. The Old and New Testaments should not be regarded as truth themselves, but as textbooks which teach the truth. Therefore, as with a textbook, they should not be regarded as absolute in every detail.[27]

e. All Christians who reject the *Divine Principle* and Sun Myung Moon will probably go to hell.[28] Indeed, they are like the Jewish chief priests and teachers of the law who persecuted Jesus.[29]

C. Refutation of Arguments Used by the Unification Church to Support Its Position on Divine Revelation

1. The *Divine Principle* contains errors.

   a. The Unification Church has had to revise the *Divine Principle* because of theological problems in previous editions that were difficult to defend. If the *Divine Principle* were truly the inspired word of God, there would have been no need to correct its errors.

   b. Unification officials argue that the problems occurred because of human error, not because God's revelations to Moon were imperfect; transcribers and translators of earlier editions did not accurately communicate Moon's teachings.[30]

   c. The problems, however, were not only textual, but also theological. The alterations between various Korean and English translations indicate a theology that has changed and continues to change.

2. The Unification Church restricts the *Divine Principle*'s distribution.

   a. If the *Divine Principle* were truly God's revealed word, God would want everyone to have the opportunity to read it.

   b. Unification theologians assert that most people would misunderstand the *Divine Principle* and reject the truth. They say that people must become aware of the truth in stages as they mature spiritually.

   c. However, the apostles and early church leaders could have said the same thing, since so many people violently opposed the Gospel. Believers do not need to manipulate God's Word to bring nonbelievers into the kingdom of God.

---

[26]Young Oon Kim, *Unification Theology* (New York: The Holy Spirit Association for the Unification of World Christianity, 1980), 50.

[27]*Divine Principle*, 9.

[28]*Divine Principle*, 535. The Unification understanding of hell is discussed at VI.B., but it should be noted here that Moon teaches that hell is not eternal.

[29]*Divine Principle*, 533.

[30]Dan Fefferman, Midwest regional director of the Unification Church, offered this explanation to me when I discussed the issue with him on a radio program in Chicago in 1977.

3. Scripture is not a textbook that teaches the truth, but is the inspired Word of God.

   a. Psalm 119:142, 151, 160: The psalmist insisted that God's "law is true" (v. 142), God's "commands are true" (v. 151), and God's "words are true" (v. 160); that is, what God has spoken is truth.

   b. John 17:17: Jesus affirmed the psalmist when he prayed, "Sanctify them by the truth; your word is truth."

   c. Matthew 5:18: Jesus said "the smallest letter" (every detail) of God's Word is to remain an absolute standard by which believers are to live.

   d. 2 Timothy 3:16: The Apostle Paul wrote that "*all* Scripture is God-breathed" (emphasis added); that is, inspired by God.

   e. 2 Peter 1:20–21: Peter provided further explanation of the process by which God conveyed Scripture: "No prophecy of Scripture came about by the prophet's own interpretation. For prophecy never had its origin in the will of man, but men spoke from God as they were carried along by the Holy Spirit."

4. Christians who reject Moon and his teachings will not go to hell.

   a. Romans 8:1: Paul affirmed that Christians will go to heaven when he wrote, "There is now no condemnation for those who are in Christ Jesus."

   b. Matthew 24:4–5: Jesus warned his followers about people like Moon: "Watch out that no one deceives you. For many will come in my name, claiming, 'I am the Christ.'"

   c. Acts 4:12: Peter declared that salvation is in Christ *alone* when he said, "Salvation is found in no one else, for there is no other name under heaven given to men by which we must be saved."

D. Arguments Used to Prove the Biblical Doctrine of Divine Revelation

1. The Bible says that a true prophet of God speaks consistently with what has already been spoken by God.

   a. The Bible condemns those who contradict God's Word.

      (1) Isaiah 8:20: The prophet Isaiah instructed the Jews: "To the law and to the testimony [that is, God's Word]! If they do not speak according to this word, they have no light of dawn."

      (2) Galatians 1:6–9: Paul was even more severe with the Galatians, who had turned to a different gospel, one that perverted the gospel of Christ.

   b. The *Divine Principle* does not merely expand upon Scripture to support Moon's theology: it contradicts the Bible in many places.

      (1) For example, the *Divine Principle* teaches that God did not originally plan for Jesus to die on the cross.[31] Peter, however,

---

[31]*Divine Principle*, 142–43; 520.

declared that Jesus of Nazareth "was handed over to you by God's set purpose and foreknowledge; and you, with the help of wicked men, put him to death by nailing him to the cross" (Acts 2:23).

(2) James Sire, in his classic book, *Scripture Twisting*, mentions another way Moon distorts Scripture: "Occasionally, Moon's ideas parallel traditional Christianity, and his use of Scripture is legitimate, but in his treatment of biblical characters such as Noah, Abraham, Moses, John the Baptist and Jesus, and their relation to his system, Moon simply ignores the obvious meanings of the biblical texts and substitutes his own."[32]

2. The Bible condemns false teachers, who try to persuade others that their teachings are the truth.

   a. Colossians 2:8: Paul told Christians to beware of the deception of people who try to captivate believers with a philosophy based on human ideas.

   b. 2 Peter 2:1–3: Peter condemned false teachers who spread destructive heresies, which deny Christ and try to exploit believers with lies.

   c. The *Divine Principle* contradicts the New Testament teachings about Christ and the essential doctrines of Scripture.

3. God's revelation in Scripture is sufficient.

   a. 2 Peter 1:3: Peter said that God "has given us *everything we need* for life and godliness through our knowledge of him."

    b. 2 Timothy 3:16–17: The "knowledge" Peter spoke of comes through Scripture, for "all Scripture is God-breathed and is useful ... so that the [person] of God may be thoroughly equipped for every good work."

   c. Luke 16:29: In the parable of the rich man and Lazarus, when the rich man asked Abraham to send Lazarus back from the afterlife to his family, Jesus indicated that Scripture was sufficient.

   d. John 5:39–40: Jesus also implied Scripture's sufficiency concerning what we need to know about him.

4. The Bible is God's revelation for all time.

   a. Psalm 119

      (1) "I learned from your statutes that you established them [God's Word] to last forever" (v. 152).

      (2) "Your word, O Lord, is eternal" (v. 89).

      (3) "All your words are true; all your righteous laws are eternal" (v. 160).

---

[32]James Sire, *Scripture Twisting* (Downers Grove, Ill.: InterVarsity Press, 1981), 133.

b. Matthew 5:17–18: Thus, since God's Word is eternal and perfect, it does not need to be replaced or changed or embellished. The New Testament extends and fulfills the Old Testament, it does not replace or change it.

II. The Doctrine of Sin

A. *The Unification Church's Position on Sin Briefly Stated*

1. Although all people want to do and pursue good, Satan, as an evil force, drives them to perform evil acts.

2. When Satan sexually seduced Eve humanity became spiritually corrupt.

3. When Adam and Eve had sexual relations against God's will, humanity became physically corrupt.

4. Spiritual and physical corruption keep humanity under the dominion of Satan and outside the providence of God.

B. *Arguments Used by the Unification Church to Support Its Position on Sin*[33]

1. David Kim, president of Unification Theological Seminary, states that contrary to what Christians have previously written, "the Unification Principle [that is, *Divine Principle*] … explains and clarifies the true story of the fall of man."

2. God created the universe and humanity to establish his kingdom on earth. In fact, God's kingdom in heaven can be realized only after the realization of God's kingdom on earth.

3. God originally intended Adam and Eve to mature to spiritual perfection before they united sexually, bore sinless offspring, and established the Kingdom of Heaven on earth. At that point they would attain deity.

4. Another created being, the angel Lucifer, thwarted God's plan.

a. He saw Eve's incredible beauty and God's deep love for Adam and Eve. Thus, because of his physical lust for her and his jealousy of God's special love for her, Lucifer desired to seduce Eve—to enjoy her physically and to grieve God spiritually.

b. Lucifer seduced Eve and had sexual relations with her.

c. In the garden of Eden, the fulfillment of Lucifer's evil intent not only caused his infamous fall, in which he became the devil, Satan, but also the spiritual fall of humanity, in which the spiritual nature of humanity was corrupted, and thus inclined toward rebellion against God.

---

[33]*Divine Principle*, 65–97.

5. Eve's sin with Lucifer made her aware of how she had deviated from God's plan.

   a. Eve realized that her divinely intended husband was to be the man Adam, not the angel Lucifer.

   b. Eve's illicit relationship with the angel disrupted God's plan.

   c. In an attempt to correct her damaged condition, Eve seduced Adam. She thought that if she began a husband and wife relationship with Adam, whom God had intended to be her husband, she would get back on track with God's plan and thus avoid God's anger.

   d. Because Adam and Eve were still spiritually immature, their union further deviated from God's plan and constituted the physical fall of humanity, in which the physical nature of humanity was corrupted, and thus made vulnerable to disease, aging, and physical death.

   e. The fact that Adam and Eve covered the parts of their bodies that they were ashamed of proves that their sin was sexual in nature.

6. Humanity must be redeemed both spiritually and physically in order for the kingdom of God to be established on earth.

   a. Thus the ultimate purpose of God's plan of salvation is to establish his kingdom on earth.

   b. Jesus Christ has accomplished *spritual redemption* in that his death on the cross has made the spirits of God's people holy before God.

   c. The Lord of the Second Advent will accomplish *physical redemption* by making the physical bodies of God's people holy before God.

   d. Physical redemption is possible for people because the Lord of the Second Advent has restored the kingdom of heaven on earth by establishing his family on earth.

      (1) The Unification Church teaches that another sinless person will become the second Messiah, or Lord of the Second Advent.

      (2) Most members believe Moon is the Lord of the Second Advent. They view Moon and his wife and children as sinless: "Father [Moon] is sinless, Mother [Moon's wife] is sinless, and their children are sinless."[34]

   e. People become physically redeemed through the accomplishments of the Lord of the Second Advent and through their own accomplishments in establishing God's kingdom on earth.[35]

---

[34]Ken Sudo, "Christology," from the *120-Day Training Manual* (n.d.), 236.

[35]The details of how this is accomplished are discussed more fully in point III.B.2.

C. Refutation of Arguments Used by the Unification Church to Support Its Position on Sin

1. The Bible does not say that Adam and Eve had to mature to spiritual perfection before they could become husband and wife. An important question that must be asked is: What is "spiritual perfection"?

   a. If spiritual perfection is a state of sinlessness, then Adam and Eve were that way when God created them; they did not become sinners until after they disobeyed God. Moon's teachings in the *Divine Principle* offer no other possible definitions for spiritual perfection.

   b. The Bible describes no conditions necessary in order for Adam and Eve to be husband and wife.

2. The Bible nowhere says that God intended for Adam and Eve to become gods.

   a. In fact, the serpent's temptation to Eve was to "be like God" (Gen. 3:5).

   b. Whenever people tried to elevate themselves to God's level, the Lord severely punished them (see Gen. 11:1–9; Isa. 14:12–15; Acts 12:21–23).

3. The Bible does not teach that the devil seduced Eve sexually.

   a. Eve's sin was that she ate the fruit from the tree of the knowledge of good and evil, which God had forbidden her to do (Gen. 3:6), not that she had an illicit love affair with Lucifer.

   b. When God asked Eve what she had done, she replied that she had eaten the fruit (v. 13).

4. The Bible never describes the sexual relationship between Adam and Eve as sin.

   a. The sin in the Garden had nothing whatever to do with sex. The Bible is explicit about what had occurred: Adam said to the Lord, "She gave me some fruit from the tree, and I ate it" (3:12).

   b. The only reference to Adam and Eve's sexual relationship was after God had pronounced his judgment on them and had driven them out of Eden. The reference records the birth of their first child (4:1). There is no reference to sexual immorality.

   c. The Bible says that Adam and Eve tried to hide their nakedness from God (3:10), and that the "garments of skin" which God made for them were meant to clothe them (3:20). It does not say that they were ashamed of any specific parts of their bodies.

5. The Bible does not assign the spiritual part of the fall to Eve's sin and the physical part to Adam's sin.

    a. Cult apologists Robert and Gretchen Passantino point out that "the Bible makes no distinction between atonement for spiritual sin and atonement for physical sin."[36]

    b. Although there were two distinct acts of disobedience on the parts of Adam and Eve, biblical writers refer to their sins as a corporate (one representing all) transgression of God's command.

    c. Romans 5:12—"Sin entered the world through one man."

        (1) Paul went on to mention Adam (v. 14), and yet it was Eve who sinned first.

        (2) Paul combined their two sins because both transgressions together constituted humanity's original sin.

        (3) If Paul was limiting his statement to only one aspect of the Fall, he should have referred to Eve's act rather than Adam's, to be consistent with Moon's theology. That is, since Paul is talking about what *Christ* accomplished toward our redemption, he should have spoken about Christ abolishing what *Eve* had done, since, in Moon's theology, Christ abolished only the results of the spiritual fall, which Eve caused, not Adam. Yet Paul talks about how Christ abolished what *Adam* had done.

  6. An official study document of the Commission on Faith and Order of the National Council of the Churches of Christ in the U.S.A. states: "The fall of man is explained [by the Unification Church] in a way which is incompatible with the Bible and Christian theology."[37]

D. Arguments Used to Prove the Biblical Doctrine of Sin

  1. Everyone is a sinner.

    a. The Bible teaches that we all have a sinful nature and commit sin.

        (1) 1 Kings 8:46—"There is no one who does not sin."

        (2) Ecclesiastes 7:20—"There is not a righteous man on earth who does what is right and never sins."

        (3) Romans 3:12—"There is no one who does good, not even one."

        (4) Galatians 3:22—"The Scripture declares that the whole world is a prisoner of sin."

        (5) 1 John 1:8, 10—"If we claim to be without sin, we deceive ourselves and the truth is not in us. ... If we claim we have not sinned, we make him [God] out to be a liar and his word has no place in our lives."

---

[36]Robert and Gretchen Passantino, *Answers to the Cultists at Your Door* (Eugene, Ore.: Harvest House, 1981), 131.

[37]"A Critique of the Theology of the Unification Church as Set Forth in *Divine Principle*," *Occasional Bulletin* (July 1977), 22.

     b. Moon suffers from a sinful nature, and therefore, he cannot be the Messiah.

  2. We are born sinful because of Adam's original sin.[38]

     a. Romans 5:12–19: Adam's transgression brought sin and condemnation into the world. We are all sinners because of Adam's disobedience.

     b. Psalm 51:5: We are not only born sinful, we are sinful from the point of our conception.

  3. Jesus Christ was without sin, though he was tempted in all things as we are (Heb. 4:15).

     a. Only Jesus Christ was, and is, without sin.

     b. Unlike all other descendants of Adam and Eve, Mary conceived Jesus through the power of the Holy Spirit, and therefore Jesus was always "holy" (Luke 1:35).

  4. Sin separates people from God.

     a. Proverbs 15:29: The Lord is far from the wicked. God loves righteousness but hates wickedness (Ps. 45:7).

     b. Romans 6:23: Even those who have eternal life are sinners.

     c. Matthew 25:31–46: Unrepentant sinners will go to hell and suffer eternal punishment (cf. Dan. 12:2).

     d. 2 Thessalonians 1:8–9: God will punish those who reject the gospel with everlasting destruction and will shut them out from his presence.

     e. Since the parents of Sun Myung Moon were both human, Moon was born sinful just like everyone else. Unless he is redeemed in Christ, he will be eternally separated from God.

III. The Doctrine of Salvation

A. The Unification Church's Position on Salvation Briefly Stated

  1. Although humanity needs to be redeemed both spiritually and physically, Jesus Christ only redeemed humanity spiritually.

  2. Therefore, a second Messiah, the Lord of the Second Advent, must come and redeem humanity physically.

  3. Humanity's physical redemption will bring about the Kingdom of Heaven on earth.

  4. The Lord of the Second Advent is Sun Myung Moon, who is in the process of fulfilling the fourfold purpose as the present Messiah by perfecting himself, his family, his nation, and the world.

---

[38]For further study on the doctrine of Original Sin, see chapter 29 of Millard J. Erickson's *Christian Theology* (Grand Rapids: Baker, 1983), 621–39.

5. Humanity must accomplish its portion of responsibility in order to be restored to God's dominion.

B. Arguments Used by the Unification Church to Support Its Position on Salvation

1. Jesus failed to fulfill God's primary purpose for humanity: to set up the Kingdom of Heaven on earth.

   Since the fall of Adam and Eve, God has been working to restore the Kingdom of Heaven on earth.[39]

   a. God prepared for Jesus' ministry by sending religious leaders around the world about four to five centuries in advance to make all peoples ready for the Messiah, who was to set up God's earthly kingdom.[40]

      (1) Malachi's prophecies were intended to reform Israel and prepare it for the coming of the Messiah.

      (2) Gautama the Buddha not only tried to improve Hinduism, but in so doing began a new world religion that eventually swept throughout Asia.

      (3) Socrates was the father of Greek philosophy. His philosophy spread throughout Europe and the Roman Empire.

      (4) Confucius taught a set of ethics and morality that became the tradition of China and other Asian nations.

   b. The followers of all these religions and philosophies were to unite under a single ruler—the Messiah.

   c. Jesus came to establish the Kingdom of Heaven on earth.[41]

      (1) Jesus was supposed to redeem humanity both in spirit and body.[42]

      (2) According to God's plan of redemption, Jesus was to accomplish God's fundamental purpose, which was to marry and bear children.[43]

         (a) In doing so, Jesus would redeem humanity both spiritually and physically.

         (b) "Unification thought diametrically contradicts the Fundamentalist view," said Young Oon Kim, "that Jesus' sole mission was to atone for the sins of mankind by dying on the cross."[44]

   d. The Jews' unbelief caused Jesus' death.

---

[39]*Divine Principle*, 140.

[40]Ibid., 423.

[41]Ibid., 140.

[42]Ibid., 147.

[43]Ibid., 152.

[44]Young Oon Kim, *Unification Theology*, 164.

(1) God had chosen the Jewish people to fulfill his plan of redemption, but they failed to carry out their responsibility to follow Jesus as the Messiah.[45]

(2) John the Baptist was responsible for the Jews' rejection of Jesus as the Messiah.[46]

Jesus had chosen John the Baptist as his main disciple, but John failed to carry out his mission to serve and minister to Jesus, so Jesus selected Peter in his place. Also, John was supposed to stand in Elijah's place and usher in the coming Messiah, but he denied that he was Elijah until his last moment, thus causing disbelief of Jesus as the Messiah among many Jews. In fact, when he was in prison, John publicly expressed his doubts about Jesus being the Messiah. Since the Jews, especially the Jewish leaders, had profound faith in John, his disbelief further caused their disbelief. "John proved to be 'an offense' to Jesus, a stumbling block in the way of realizing the kingdom."[47]

(3) The Jews' disbelief forced Jesus to choose the way of the cross, which would redeem humanity spiritually but not physically.[48]

e. Jesus' death on the cross meant that he could not fulfill the total redemption of humanity.

(1) It is obvious that Christ's crucifixion did not remove original sin since the followers of Christ still sin.[49] Although Christians are spiritually redeemed, they are still subject to sin in their flesh.

(2) Even Jesus said that the Lord must come again to complete humanity's restoration to its original state of sinlessness.[50]

(3) Thus Jesus failed to establish the kingdom of Heaven on earth because he did not redeem humanity physically.[51]

2. The Lord of the Second Advent will establish the kingdom of Heaven on earth by redeeming humanity physically.

a. When the Lord of the Second Advent will come

(1) There were two thousand years between Adam and Abraham during which God laid the foundation for his people, Israel.[52]

---

[45]*Divine Principle*, 371

[46]*Divine Principle,* 157–62

[47]Young Oon Kim, *Unification Theology,* 151.

[48]*Divine Principle,* 151.

[49]Ibid., 142.

[50]Ibid., 142.

[51]Ibid., 147.

[52]Ibid., 173, 231.

31

  (2) There were two thousand years between Abraham and Jesus, the second Adam, during which time Israel was to prepare for the coming of the Messiah.[53]

  (3) There will be two thousand years between Jesus and the Lord of the Second Advent, the third Adam, during which time Christians are to lay the groundwork for the coming of the second Messiah.[54]

  (4) Therefore we know that now is the time for the Christ to come again.[55]

 b. Where the Lord of the Second Advent will come from

  (1) Revelation 7:2–4 says an angel will come from the east with the seal of God, and he will seal God's chosen servants.[56]

  (2) From these verses, it can be determined that the Lord of the Second Advent will be born in a country in the East.[57]

  (3) From ancient times, Japan, China, and Korea have been referred to as the "Eastern nations."[58]

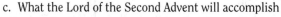

  Japan is a country that worships pagan gods, and therefore is not a suitable birthplace for the Messiah. China is a communist country that persecutes Christians and therefore is not a suitable birthplace for the Messiah.[59] The Korean people, however, are on the "Heavenly side" because they are endowed with a strong faith in God that makes Korea a suitable birthplace for the Messiah.[60] Therefore, the Lord of the Second Advent will come from Korea.[61]

 c. What the Lord of the Second Advent will accomplish

  (1) He will perfect himself by defeating (that is, subjugating) Satan.[62]

  He will be born on earth, in the flesh,[63] and will remove himself from Satan's lineage.[64] (All descendants of Eve are said to be included in Satan's lineage because of her sexual intercourse with him. The Lord of the Second Advent removes himself from Satan's lineage when he resists Satan's influence and

---

[53]Ibid., 232, 430.
[54]Ibid., 232, 499.
[55]Ibid., 498–99.
[56]Ibid., 519.
[57]Ibid., 520.
[58]Ibid.
[59]Ibid.
[60]Ibid., 526–27.
[61]Ibid., 520.
[62]Ibid., 180.
[63]Ibid., 364.
[64]Ibid., 368–69.

subjects himself totally to God's will.) Also, this time the Messiah will not come to die, though Christians will persecute him because of their disbelief.[65]

(2) He will perfect his family.[66]

He will complete his mission by having a wife.[67]

Their children (twelve living at this time) will not only represent, but actually stand in the place of the twelve tribes of Israel and Jesus' twelve apostles.[68] Moreover, Heung Jin Nim, Sun Myung Moon's son who died in a traffic accident in Poughkeepsie, New York on January 2, 1984, carries on his father's work in heaven. The spirits of deseased people "all refer to Heung Jin Nim as the new Christ. [Unificationists say he is the heavenly Christ while Moon is the earthly Christ.] They also call him the youth-king of heaven. He is the King of Heaven in the spirit world. Jesus is working with him and always accompanies him. ... How could he reach such a high position? He didn't live long on earth. He was still a student when he died at the age of seventeen. ... Heung Jin Nim gained this position because he died in Father's place. ... It is a great blessing for us to have Father on earth and Heung Jin Nim doing Father's work in the spirit world."[69]

(3) He will perfect his nation.[70]

Korea is the battleground between good and evil. In fact, the 38th parallel is the line that divides democracy and communism but it also separates God and Satan.[71] The democratic world belongs to God, for democracy represents the heavenly principles of God,[72] while the communist world belongs to Satan, for communism represents the demonic principles of Satan.[73] The Korean people will win the final victory over communism as the nation on the heavenly side.[74]

(4) He will perfect the world.[75]

[65]Ibid., 364–65.

[66]Ibid., 187.

[67]Ibid., 152.

[68]Ibid., 379, 382.

[69]Young Whi Kim, *Guidance for Heavenly Tradition*, vol. 2 (Mainz, Germany: Vereinigungskirche, 1985), 183–84.

[70]*Divine Principle*, 521.

[71]Ibid., 524.

[72]Ibid., 480.

[73]Ibid., 125.

[74]Ibid., 527.

[75]Ibid., 187.

All religions will finally be unified when they recognize and serve the Lord of the Second Advent.[76] After the communist world of Satan is subjugated, all nations will be united into one kingdom on earth, centered on God,[77] and ultimately, everyone will recognize and serve the Lord of the Second Advent.[78] In other words, through a process of obedience to the Lord of the Second Advent in which followers accomplish specific goals, such as converting a certain number of people and marrying within the Unification Church (or having their marriage blessed by Moon), Moon's followers become perfect.

3. Is Sun Myung Moon the Lord of the Second Advent?

    a. Nowhere in the *Divine Principle* does Moon claim to be the Messiah.

    b. However, most members in the Unification Church believe that Moon is the Lord of the Second Advent when it describes from where and when the second Messiah will come and what he must accomplish.

        (1) Though not stated explicitly, the *Divine Principle* clearly points to Moon as the Lord of the Second Advent.

        (2) Other teaching materials, such as the "Sermons of Rev. Moon" and leadership training manuals, speak more clearly of Moon as the Messiah.

        (3) Unification Church members believe that Moon is in the process of fulfilling the work of the Lord of the Second Advent. In fact, leaders in the Unification Church, such as Ken Sudo, boldly teach that "Rev. Moon is the Messiah, the Lord of the Second Advent."[79]

        (4) After Jesus asked Moon to complete the work of redemption which he had left unfinished and Moon accepted this mission to redeem humanity, Moon battled with Satan for nine years until he subjugated Satan. Satan tried to discourage Moon by tempting him to sin or to feel he was not strong enough to fulfill God's plan, but finally gave up.[80]

        (5) Moon's wife has given birth to thirteen children (one died in an accident), thus fulfilling the number of spiritual completion, that is, twelve.

        (6) Although communism still survives in many parts of the world—especially in North Korea—there are obvious signs

---

[76]Ibid., 190.

[77]Ibid., 474.

[78]Ibid., 190.

[79]Sudo, "Family Problems," from the *120-Day Training Manual* (n.d.), 160.

[80]Sun Myung Moon, *Message to the World Unification Family,* sermon (Washington, D.C.: The Holy Spirit Association for the Unification of World Christianity, 1964), 4.

that this demonic philosophy is dying. (Note, for example, the fall of communism in the former Soviet Union and Eastern Europe.)

(7) It might seem to some that the world is far from unifying both religiously and politically, and that few recognize Moon as the Messiah, but the seeds for his lordship have been planted throughout the world, especially in the United States.

4. The doctrine of indemnity

a. Indemnity is that which people do to restore themselves to God's kingdom.

b. Young Oon Kim describes it this way: "We atone for our sins through specific acts of penance."[81]

c. Kwang-Yol Yoo, a Unification teacher, even goes so far as to say that by following the *Divine Principle*, "man's perfection must be accomplished finally by his own effort without God's help."[82]

d. God does most of the work, but people must still do their part in order to achieve God's plan of salvation: "Five percent is only to say that man's reponsibility is extremely small compared to God's."[83]

C. Refutation of Arguments Used by the Unification Church to Support Its Position on Salvation

1. Jesus did not fail to accomplish his mission.

Jesus and the New Testament writers taught that Jesus fully redeemed God's chosen people. (See D.3. below.)

2. God was not preparing the world through other religions.

a. Outside of Judaism, no religion or philosophy taught their believers that a messiah or Christ would come to forgive their sins, which was Jesus' primary earthly ministry.

b. Gautama the Buddha taught that to believe in any god actually hinders one's attainment of spiritual enlightenment.

c. The major teachers of classical Hinduism taught that the ultimate spiritual goal is to lose one's identity and become one with the cosmic universe.

d. Confucius and the Greek philosophers were more concerned about people's ethical relationships with one another and the state than with their moral obligation to an absolute God.

3. The nations and religions of the world will never willingly unite.

a. There is too much hatred for one another for them to unite—even for their own good.

---

[81]Young Oon Kim, *Unification Theology*, 230.

[82]"Unification Church History from the Early Days," *New Hope News* (October 7, 1974), 7.

[83]*Divine Principle*, 198.

    b. Moreover, their goals and ambitions are contrary to the teachings of Christ.

    c. Furthermore, it is arguable whether global cooperation is increasing.

4. Although the defeat of communism illustrates God's judgment against an evil institution, it does not mean that evil has been defeated absolutely.[84]

    a. A vivid example of this is in the former nation of Yugoslavia, where a worse evil has emerged from the ashes of communism.

    b. Indeed, it was, arguably, communist rule that had kept ancient racial hatreds in check.

    c. The defeat of communism in Korea does not mean that Korea will be a godly country, particularly since so much evil has already been committed in democratic South Korea.

5. Jesus said that the Kingdom of Heaven had already come.

    a. When Jesus spoke of the kingdom of God, at certain occasions he indicated it had already come by his presence.

      (1) Jesus told the Pharisees that his casting out demons was proof that God's kingdom had come (Matt. 12:28; Luke 11:20).

      (2) Jesus sent out his disciples to prepare for his coming and proclaim that God's kingdom was near (Luke 10:1–9).

    b. Jesus never said he would establish the kingdom of Heaven on earth by marrying someone and producing children.

      (1) Mark 2:18–22: Cult apologist Bryce Pettit makes the point that "a marriage motif is almost completely lacking in Jesus' early teaching ministry, and where it does come up, it contains an allusion to his death!"[85]

      (2) Luke 10:1–11: Jesus commissioned his disciples to go out before him to proclaim the coming of God's kingdom; that is, Jesus himself.

      (3) John 18:36: Jesus told Pilate that his kingdom was of another world, and if he wanted to, he could have his servants fight to protect him.

      (4) Jesus didn't have to marry and raise children in order to set up God's heavenly kingdom on earth; the presence of God's king-

---

[84]Interestingly, "the largest number of Unification workshops in history was held in the former Soviet Union last year [1992]. According to an article in the Oct./Nov. 1992 issue of *Today's World* [a Unification publication], Unificationist training workshops were held for 18,042 students and teachers from Russian high schools and universities." Unification teachers answered their questions about Moon, saying "'Yes, Rev. Moon is the Messiah,' and explained why." The Unification Church also has the strong support of such Russian officials as the president of Lithuania, and *Isvestia*, a major Russian newspaper, has translated the *Divine Principle* into Russian. One copy of the *Divine Principle* was given to each participant. See Eric Pement, "Moon over Moscow," *Cornerstone* Vol. 22, no. 101 (1993), 19, 21.

[85]*Contend for the Faith*, ed. Eric Pement (Chicago: Evangelical Ministries to New Religions, 1992), 166.

dom was already present in Jesus, and he could establish it anytime and anywhere he desired.

    (5) Jesus never showed any signs that he was looking for a wife, despite being surrounded by many respected female admirers, such as Martha and Mary, the sisters of his dear friend Lazarus.

  c. Although some Jews did not believe that Jesus was the Messiah and even plotted his death, many Jews did become his faithful followers.

    (1) All of his closest followers and leaders of the early church were Jews.

    (2) Indeed, some of his followers were highly respected leaders in the Jewish community, such as Nicodemus and Joseph of Arimathea.

    (3) Since God is all-powerful, and since many Jews were strong supporters of Jesus, certainly Jesus could have set up an earthly kingdom if that had been God's primary plan.

6. The Jews did not stumble over the alleged faithlessness of John the Baptist.

  a. The same Jewish leaders who rejected Jesus also had rejected John throughout his ministry and John rebuked them for their hypocrisy.

  b. John always pointed the people to Jesus as the Savior (e.g., John 1:15–34).

  c. John had not failed in his mission. In fact, Jesus said of John after his death, "I tell you the truth: Among those born of women there has not risen anyone greater than John the Baptist. . . . He is the Elijah who was to come" (Matt. 11:11, 14).

7. The sins of Christians do not negate the completed work of Christ's redemption on the cross.

  a. The Bible acknowledges that those who are in Christ still sin during their earthly lives (Gal. 2:17; 1 John 1:8, 10).

  b. Nevertheless, even though Christians sin, Christ's sacrifice still made Christians "perfect forever" (Heb. 10:14).

8. Jesus did not die because of circumstances beyond his control.

  a. It was *God's* plan that the Messiah die for people's sins.

    (1) Matthew 26:42: Jesus indicated in his prayer in the garden of Gethsemane that it was his Father's will for him to die.

    (2) Luke 24:25: Jesus rebuked the two men going to Emmaus for despairing over Jesus' death and seeming disappearance. He told them that his death was prophetically ordained according to God's plan.

    (3) Hebrews 10:5–10: It was God's will that Jesus Christ die for our sins.

(4) 1 John 4:10: John wrote: "This is love: not that we loved God, but that he loved us and sent his Son as an atoning sacrifice for our sins."

(5) Acts 2:23: Peter was even more explicit: "This man [Jesus of Nazareth] was handed over to you by God's set purpose and foreknowledge; and you, with the help of wicked men, put him to death by nailing him to the cross."

b. It was *Jesus'* plan to die for people's sins.

(1) Philippians 2:6–8: Jesus obeyed his heavenly Father by becoming a human being and even dying on the cross.

(2) Matthew 26:42: Jesus chose to submit to God's will and to die for sinners rather than to let "the cup" pass.

(3) John 10:18: Christ laid down his life of his own accord; he had the power both to lay it down and to take it up again (cf. John 2:19).

(4) Jesus chose to take the path of the cross before he was born on earth and continued to choose that path while he lived on earth.

c. At the height of Jesus' popularity, he told his followers that he had to go to Jerusalem to die (Matt. 16:21).

(1) This shows that Jesus did not embrace death because he had no other alternative.

(2) When Jesus ministered publicly in Jerusalem, his enemies were afraid to do anything against him because he had the support of the people (Luke 19:48; 20:19).

(3) Jesus' enemies had to arrest and try him quickly and at night in secret before the Jewish people could protest (Luke 22:53).

9. The *Divine Principle*'s description of the Messiah's Second Advent is illogical.

a. Moon's end-time chronology is absurd.

(1) It is arbitrary to assume that 2000 years is the critical number used to determine when the Second Coming will occur.

(2) Even if one grants that 2000 years is such a critical number in determining the Second Coming, Moon's chronology still is incorrect.

For example, it is quite doubtful that God called Abraham exactly 2000 years after Adam's creation. More importantly, 2000 years have not transpired since Jesus' birth, and yet members of the Unification Church believe the Lord of the Second Advent came over fifty years ago, when Moon accepted the alleged call from Jesus to save the world.

b. Moon's claim that a second Messiah must come from Korea is illogical.

(1) Moon's explanation of the fulfillment of Revelation 7:2–4 is incomprehensible.

(2) The most astounding interpretation of these verses is that the second Messiah will be born in Korea because the angel descended from the east.

(3) Moon's interpretation makes a number of incredible assumptions:

    (a) that the second Messiah will be born in an Eastern country when "the east" mentioned in Revelation refers only to direction

    (b) that only Japan, China, and Korea are Eastern countries when there are many other Eastern countries

    (c) that only Korea has a holy people, making it a worthy birthplace for the second Messiah when Korea has more Buddhists than Christians

10. Sun Myung Moon could not be the Messiah.

    a. Even if one grants the Unification picture of the Messiah, Moon does not meet his own requirements.

        (1) Moon teaches that, whereas the Lord of the First Advent was a suffering servant, the Lord of the Second Advent will come as a triumphant king, but this does not fit with claims of his "martyrdom."

        On the one hand, the Unificationists revere Moon as a martyr who was cruelly tortured by the communists, unjustly imprisoned by the United States government, and constantly persecuted by Christians. On the other hand, Moon presents himself as a triumphant king. Therefore, Moon must decide whether he wants to be a martyr (like the Lord of the First Advent) or the triumphant king (like the Lord of the Second Advent). To be consistent with his own theology he cannot be both.

        (2) The most visible proof that Moon has not perfected his family will be when the actions of his children, who are supposed to be sinless, become publicly known.

        Up to this date, little has been said about Moon's children in the news media because they have been carefully sequestered.

        As time goes by, however, especially after Moon's eventual death, they will no doubt demonstrate that they are not sinless.

    b. Moon's claim that he received truth from past spiritual leaders shows that he is not the Messiah.

        (1) Moon asserts that prior to defeating Satan, great spiritual leaders of the past (including Christ) imparted truth to him.

(2) Jesus Christ, however, did not gain truth from other people; he said he (as God) was the truth (John 14:6).

11. The doctrine of indemnity is not biblical.

a. "In simple language," states Ruth Tucker, "indemnity is salvation by works."[86]

b. Bob Larson makes a distinction between Moon's doctrine and biblical theology, saying, "Moon's doctrine of sinless perfection by 'indemnity' [forgiveness of sin by works on Moon's behalf], which can apply even to deceased ancestors, is a denial of the salvation by grace offered through Christ."[87]

c. "Farewell," said John Calvin, "to the dream of those who think up a righteousness flowing together out of faith and works."[88]

D. Arguments Used to Prove the Biblical Doctrine of Salvation

1. The Second Coming of Christ is the return of Jesus, not another person.

a. The Bible clearly states that the *very same* Jesus who came the first time will come again (Acts 1:11; 1 Thess. 1:10; Titus 2:11–14; Rev. 22:12–16) and will be revealed at that coming (1 Cor. 1:7; 2 Thess. 1:6–7; 1 Peter 1:7, 13).

(1) Jesus referred to himself as "the Son of Man" eighty-one times in the Gospels (e.g., Matt. 26:1–2; Mark 14:60–62).

(2) Among these references Jesus explicitly said *he* would return (Matt. 16:27; 25:31; Mark 8:38; 13:26; Luke 17:30).

b. When Jesus does return, he will not be born into this world a second time, but will appear in the sky.

(1) Paul told the Thessalonians that when Christ returns he will descend from heaven in the clouds (1 Thess. 4:16–17; cf. Dan. 7:13; Rev. 1:7).

(2) Jesus described in detail how he will come on the clouds of the sky with his angels (Matt. 24:30–31; Mark 13:26–27).

(3) When Jesus ascended into heaven, angels told his followers that "this same Jesus" would return in the same way (Acts 1:11).

c. Many will claim to be the Messiah but they are false Christs; Jesus warned that many would claim to be him and try to mislead people (Matthew 24:4–24).

d. No one can predict when Jesus will return.

---

[86]Tucker, 253.

[87]Bob Larson, *New Book of Cults* (Wheaton, Ill.: Tyndale House, 1992), 445.

[88]John Calvin, *Institutes of the Christian Religion* 1 (Philadelphia: Westminster, 1960), 744.

(1) Jesus said no one knows the day or hour of his return; he will come when we do not expect him (Matt. 24:36; Mark 13:32; Luke 12:40; Acts 1:6–7; Rev. 3:3; 16:15).

(2) Jesus will come like "a thief in the night" (1 Thess. 5:1–2; 2 Peter 3:10; cf. Matt. 24:44); that is, unexpectedly.

2. Jesus Christ is the only Savior.

   a. Acts 4:8–12: Peter, filled with the Holy Spirit, proclaimed to the Jewish rulers and elders that there is salvation in no one except Jesus Christ of Nazareth.

   b. John 14:6: Jesus himself declared that no one can come to the Father except through him.

3. Jesus' death on the cross provided complete redemption for our sins—physically as well as spiritually.

   a. Matthew 9:6: To prove to the teachers of the law that he had authority on earth to forgive sins, Jesus healed a paralytic, thus demonstrating that he had authority to heal both physically and spiritually.

      (1) That authority, which was demonstrated partially in the Gospels by Jesus' physical healings, will someday be totally executed in the complete "redemption of the body" (Rom. 8:23) at the believers' resurrection (John 5:25, 28–29).

      (2) It is interesting that Moon—who purportedly has accomplished much more than Jesus in terms of physically redeeming the world, such as establishing a sinless family to set up God's kingdom on earth—has not healed anyone physically.

   b. Hebrews 10:12, 14: Jesus has perfected for all time those he has saved through his death. Ultimately this perfection will include the physical as well as the spiritual.

   c. 1 Thessalonians 5:23: God will keep the believer's spirit, soul, and body (that is, the whole person) blameless at the return of Jesus Christ.

4. Christ accomplished the entire work of our salvation.

   a. We are saved by grace through faith in Christ (Eph. 2:8).

      (1) God's grace is that Jesus Christ died on our behalf and atoned for our sins so that we might know God's forgiveness (Rom. 3:24–26).

      (2) God's grace cannot be earned (Rom. 3:28).

   b. We can contribute nothing to our salvation (Eph. 2:9).

      (1) We are not justified by observing God's laws, but by putting our faith in Jesus Christ (Gal. 2:15–16).

      (2) Since Christ has done everything needed for our salvation, we have no grounds for boasting (Rom. 3:27).

41

   c. Though we are not saved *by* our good works, we are saved *in order to do* good works (Eph. 2:10).

     (1) God has predestined us to be conformed to the image of Jesus Christ (Rom. 8:29). In doing this, God is the potter and we are the clay (Isa. 64:8; Jer. 18:6; Rom. 9:20).

     (2) Our good works demonstrate the genuineness of our faith in Christ (James 2:17).

     (3) Because true faith in Christ produces obedience, our good works are a result, not a cause, of God's work in us (Rom. 1:5; Phil. 2:12–13).

IV. The Deity of Jesus Christ and the Trinity

A. The Unification Church's Position on the Deity of Jesus Christ and the Trinity Briefly Stated

  1. Jesus Christ is not God.

  2. Jesus Christ is not equal to God the Father.

  3. Jesus did attain perfection, and therefore a kind of "deity."

  4. Therefore, Jesus can, in a limited sense, be called "God."

B. Arguments Used by the Unification Church to Support Its Position on the Deity of Jesus Christ and the Trinity

  1. Christology[89]

    a. Sun Myung Moon was the first to explain accurately who Jesus was.

     (1) Until Moon, no one fully understood who Jesus really was.

     (2) The *Divine Principle* resolves the confusion concerning the Christian doctrine on Jesus Christ.

    b. God created humanity to be perfect and sinless.

     (1) The purpose of creation is for humanity to establish a perfect relationship with God.

     (2) Those who have established a perfect union with God have perfected themselves.

     (3) The first perfect human being also becomes the Tree of Life, which is a symbol of eternal life in God.[90]

     (4) If Adam had become perfect, he would have become the Tree of Life.

     (5) The one who has become perfect assumes deity.[91]

    c. Jesus became spiritually perfect, and therefore, attained deity.

---

[89]*Divine Principle*, 205–18.

[90]Ibid., 68.

[91]Ibid., 43.

      (1) Jesus, as a human being, fulfilled the purpose of creation when he became one body spiritually with God (one in the sense that Jesus had a perfect spiritual relationship with God).

      (2) Because Jesus was the first to become spiritually perfect, he became the Tree of Life (i.e., a symbol of eternal life in God).

      (3) Since Jesus became spiritually perfect, he also attained deity.

      (4) In a spiritual sense, Jesus can be called "God."

   d. Jesus, however, did not perfect himself physically because the Jewish people handed his body over to Satan to be crucified.[92]

      (1) Although Jesus accomplished the spiritual purpose of creation, he was no different from ordinary, fallen men and women in terms of his outward appearance.

      (2) According to the purpose of creation, only through the physical body can a person become totally perfect since God's plan is to establish his kingdom on earth.

      (3) Before Moon, no one has become perfect both spiritually and physically.[93]

      (4) Therefore, before Moon no one has lived a life of complete oneness with God.

   e. Jesus is not God.[94]

      (1) Jesus could not intercede on behalf of people before himself.

      (2) Jesus prayed to God, and God cannot pray to himself.

      (3) Satan tempted Jesus, and God cannot be tempted.

      (4) If Jesus were God, evil forces would not have defeated him when they crucified him.

      (5) Jesus declared that God had forsaken him on the cross, and God cannot forsake himself.

2. The Trinity[95]

   a. God's original purpose for the trinity

      (1) Originally, God's reason for creating Adam and Eve was to form a trinity by uniting them into one body with himself (where unimpeded interaction and communication could occur among the three).

      (2) Since Adam and Eve did not perfect themselves, however, they could not form the trinity.

   b. God's second attempt at forming the trinity

92*Divine Principle*, 141, 171, 173, 510–12.

93Ibid., 511.

94*Divine Principle*, 212.

95*Divine Principle*, 217–18.

(1) After Jesus perfected himself spiritually, God was able to form a spiritual trinity with Jesus and the Holy Spirit.

(2) Jesus' death on the cross prevented him from marrying, and thus God could not form a physical trinity with Jesus and the wife he might have married.

c. God's current fulfillment of the trinity

(1) The Christ must come again in the flesh to establish both the spiritual and the physical trinity.

(2) The members of the physical trinity will be God, the Lord of the Second Advent, and the Lord of the Second Advent's wife (who will not be a spiritual wife, like the Holy Spirit, but a physical wife).

(3) When the physical trinity is formed, then the kingdom of Heaven will be established on earth.

C. *Refutation of Arguments Used by the Unification Church to Support Its Position on the Deity of Jesus Christ and the Trinity*

1. Christology[96]

a. The *Divine Principle's* explanation on the deity of Jesus Christ is heretical.

(1) It contradicts the teachings of Jesus, Paul, and other New Testament writers. (See IV.D. for biblical testimony.)

(2) It conflicts with the teachings of the church, particularly as set forth at the fourth church council at Chalcedon in 451, where orthodox Christians hammered out their statement on the divine and human natures in Jesus Christ.[97]

(3) Thus, contrary to Moon's assertions, neither the New Testament writers nor orthodox Christians throughout the centuries have been confused about who Christ is.

b. Humans cannot achieve perfection through their own efforts.

(1) Because of the Fall, all humans are sinful by nature; that is, they are naturally inclined to sin (Gen. 8:21; Ps. 51:5; Rom. 3:9).

(2) Because of their sinful nature, humans do not have the ability to establish a perfect relationship with God and to perfect

---

[96]For a critique of Moon's teaching on Christology, see "Unification Church," in *Dictionary of Cults, Sects, Religions and the Occult,* eds. George A. Mather and Larry A. Nichols (Grand Rapids: Zondervan, 1993), 284.

[97]For further study on the early creeds of the Christian church, see Athanasius, *The Incarnation of the Word of God* (London: A. R. Mowbray, 1963); Gerrit Cornelis Berkouwer, *The Person of Christ* (Grand Rapids: Eerdmans, 1954); Geoffrey W. Bromiley, *Historical Theology: An Introduction* (Grand Rapids: Eerdmans, 1978); J. N. D. Kelley, *Early Christian Doctrines,* 2d ed. (New York: Harper and Row, 1960); Otto William Heick, *A History of Christian Thought,* 2 vols. (Philadelphia: Fortress, 1965); Phillip Schaff, *The Creeds of Christendom,* rep. (Grand Rapids: Baker, no copyright but published in 1965); and Reinhold Seeberg, *Text-Book of the History of Doctrines,* trans. Charles E. Hay, 2 vols. (Grand Rapids: Baker, 1961).

themselves (Job 14:4; Pss. 14:2–3; 53:2–3; Rom. 5:6–11; 7:18–19).

    (3) Nowhere in the Bible does it say Adam was intended to become the Tree of Life.

    (4) The Bible never says humans can become divine.

c. Jesus was perfect in every way.

    (1) God demonstrated his sovereign power by using even the forces of evil to accomplish his purpose at the cross; Satan did not invade Jesus' body but was decisively defeated by his perfect sacrifice.[98]

    (2) God has sovereignly used evil to accomplish his purpose (Job 1:12; 2:6; Hab. 1:6; Acts 2:22–23; 2 Cor. 12:7); it does not indicate any lack of perfection in God.

    (3) Likewise, Jesus' decision to die on the cross does not indicate a shortcoming or failure on his part (Matt. 16:21; Luke 24:25–27; Acts 2:23; 3:13–18).

    (4) Jesus was fully human in every respect (John 1:14; Phil. 2:7; Heb. 2:17), except that he was without sin (2 Cor. 5:21; Heb. 4:14–15; 7:26; 1 Peter 2:22; 1 John 3:5).[99]

d. Jesus is both fully God and fully human.

    (1) Jesus was fully human, yet without sin.

As a human being, Jesus was different from fallen humanity in that he was physically conceived through the Holy Spirit. Indeed, the angel Gabriel told Mary that the Holy Spirit would come upon her and that she would conceive and give birth to Jesus (Luke 1:35). Jesus was not only born without original sin (that is, his human nature was not tainted or corrupted by sin), but also throughout his life he did not sin (1 Peter 2:22; 1 John 3:5). Throughout his earthly existence, Jesus lived in perfect harmony with God. At the end of his earthly ministry, Jesus said, "I have obeyed my Father's commands and remain in his love" (John 15:10).

    (2) Jesus did not need to strive to become divine since he already was God (John 1:1; Rom. 9:5; Phil. 2:6–8; Col. 2:9; 2 Peter 1:1).

    (3) Jesus Christ lives forever to intercede on behalf of God's people before God the Father (Rom. 8:34; 1 Tim. 2:5; Heb. 7:23–25; 13:8; 1 John 2:1). Indeed, Christ reconciled us to God through his physical body (Col. 1:22).

---

[98]Moon teaches that when Jesus was crucified, Satan invaded his body, making Jesus unable to attain physical perfection and to remove original sin from his followers (see V.B.3.c.).

[99]Note that sin is not essential to our humanness. Adam and Eve were fully human before the Fall. Sin is a corruption of our humanness, brought about by the Fall. Therefore, there is no contradiction between describing Jesus as fully human and yet without sin.

(4) As the Son of God, Jesus could pray to God his Father.

Jesus is fully God, but he is also fully human. Therefore, as a man, he could pray to his Father. Although the Father and the Son are both fully God, the Father is not to be confused with the Son, as though they are the same person. God exists eternally as three persons. Therefore, Moon's argument that Jesus could not be God because he would be praying to himself is nonsense from a biblical, trinitarian point of view. (See point 2 below.)

(5) Jesus' temptations and sufferings must be understood in light of his humanity.

Although Satan cannot tempt God the Father (James 1:13), Satan could tempt Jesus in his human form (Luke 4:1–13). Jesus was "tempted in every way, just as we are—yet was without sin" (Heb. 4:15). Also, when Jesus cried out that God had forsaken him (Matt. 27:46; Mark 15:34), he was quoting Psalm 22:1 because at that moment he bore our sins, which God the Father could not allow in his presence.

e. The forces of evil did not defeat Jesus at the cross; rather, Jesus vanquished evil at his crucifixion and conquered the effect of sin, that is death, when he was resurrected.

(1) Colossians 2:15: Jesus triumphed over the powers of evil at the cross and made a public spectacle of them.

(2) 1 Corinthians 15:54–56: Jesus' resurrection from the dead has taken out the "sting of death" and given us victory over death.

2. The Trinity

a. Moon's "trinity" is different from the biblical doctrine.

(1) Although the Bible never uses the word *trinity*, Christians coined the term to refer to the fact that the one God exists eternally as three persons: the Father (Phil. 2:11), the Son (Heb. 1:8), and Holy Spirit (Acts 5:3–4).

Even though the word *trinity* is not in the Bible, the teaching of one God in three persons is. In response to Moon's teachings, Walter Martin made this point: "As early as the second century of the Christian Church the word *trinity* [Latin, *trinitas*] was invoked as a means of expressing the mysterious relationship extant between the Father, Christ, and the Spirit."[100]

(2) Moon, on the other hand, uses this term in a general sense to refer to the relationship between God and two perfected, married people.

---

[100]Martin, 343.

For example, Moon said if Adam and Eve had perfected themselves, they and their descendants (succeeding couples) would have formed trinities with God.[101] This use of *trinity* is utterly foreign to the biblical concept of the term.

b. God did not need to form himself as a trinity.

  (1) Scripture nowhere teaches that God attempted to form a trinity of the sort Moon describes.

  (2) Because God does not change (Mal. 3:6) he has always existed as the Trinity; God did not establish himself as a trinity.

  (3) Since "Jesus Christ is the same yesterday and today and forever" (Heb. 13:8), he did not become part of the Trinity but always was part of the Trinity.

D. Arguments Used to Prove the Biblical Doctrine of the Deity of Jesus Christ and the Trinity

1. Christology

  a. Jesus Christ is the Creator.

   (1) John 1:3: The apostle John said *all* things came into existence through Jesus Christ; he is not part of God's creation.

   (2) Colossians 1:16: The apostle Paul said all things—in heaven and on earth—were created through Jesus Christ.

   (3) Hebrews 1:2: The universe was made through Jesus, the Son of God.

  b. Jesus Christ is eternal.

   (1) Jesus did not say "Before Abraham was born, I was," but "Before Abraham was born, I am!" (John 8:58); he was not merely saying he existed before Abraham, but that he has *always* existed. The "I Am" title is taken from Exodus 3:14, where God identifies himself by this title. Therefore, Jesus was claiming to be the eternal God.

   (2) John 1:2: Jesus was with God in the beginning.

   (3) Colossians 1:17: Jesus existed before all things were created. Since Jesus is not in the class of created things, he is the Creator of all things.

  c. Jesus Christ was physically conceived in the virgin Mary through the power of the Holy Spirit.

   (1) Luke 1:31–35: The angel Gabriel announced to Mary that the Holy Spirit would come upon her, she would conceive the Son of God, and was to call him Jesus.

   (2) Matthew 1:20–23: Gabriel also told Joseph, Mary's fiancé, that Mary would bear a child, though she was a virgin, that this

---

[101]*Divine Principle*, 217.

child was conceived in Mary by the Holy Spirit, and that the child was to be called Jesus.

    (3) Isaiah 7:14: About seven centuries earlier, God had said this child would be born of a virgin.

  d. Jesus Christ is God.

    (1) John 1:1: Jesus Christ is the Word and the Word is God.

    (2) 2 Peter 1:1: Peter referred to Jesus Christ as his "God and Savior."

    (3) Colossians 2:9: All the fullness of the Deity dwells in Jesus Christ's bodily form.

    (4) Titus 2:13: Paul called Jesus Christ his "great God."

    (5) John 20:28: Upon believing in Jesus' bodily resurrection, Thomas called Jesus his Lord and God.

    (6) John 10:33: When the Jews picked up stones to stone Jesus because he claimed to be God, Jesus made no effort to refute it.

    (7) Hebrews 1:8: Even the Father called his Son "God."

2. The Trinity

  a. The distinction of the three persons of the Godhead

    (1) Luke 3:21–22: Matthew illustrated this distinction in his record of Jesus' baptism, when the Holy Spirit descended upon Jesus and the Father spoke to him from heaven.

    (2) John 16:28: At the last supper, Jesus said he had come from the Father and was returning to the Father.

    (3) John 16:7: Jesus also said the Holy Spirit (the Counselor) could not come to his disciples until he had returned to heaven. Thus Jesus taught that he, God the Father, and the Holy Spirit are personally distinct from one another.

    (4) 2 Corinthians 13:14: Paul said, "May the grace of the Lord Jesus Christ, and the love of God, and the fellowship of the Holy Spirit be with you all." This verse has been the trinitarian benediction used in Christian worship to acknowledge the Holy Trinity.

    (5) John 1:1: John said, "the Word [Jesus] was *with* God [the Father], and the Word *was* God" (emphasis added); that is, Jesus and the Father are distinct persons who share the same essence.

  b. The unity of the Godhead

    (1) Ephesians 4:4–6: Paul said there is one God, and he had proclaimed Jesus to be God (Col. 2:9; cf. 1 Cor. 8:6).

    (2) Mark 12:29: Jesus himself recited the *Shema* (the Jewish confession of faith in the one true God from Deut. 6:4).

V. The Resurrection of Jesus Christ

A. *The Unification Church's Position on the Resurrection of Jesus Christ Briefly Stated*

1. Jesus Christ was resurrected from the dead spiritually but not physically.

2. After Jesus Christ was raised from the dead, he appeared to his disciples as a transcendent being—a visible, spiritual being without a physical body.

3. The resurrection of Jesus Christ only furthers God's plan of redemption to a limited degree; it accomplished the redemption of a believer's spirit, but not his or her physical body.

B. *Arguments Used by the Unification Church to Support Its Position on the Resurrection of Jesus Christ*[102]

1. When Jesus was resurrected, he no longer possessed a physical body.

   a. No human body can be resurrected to its original form after death because it decays.

   b. After Jesus was raised from the dead, he could not be seen with physical eyes because he had become a being transcendent of the material world.

   c. "The physical resurrection and bodily ascension of Jesus ... are not an essential part of ... faith in Jesus as the risen Lord."[103]

2. The Jesus the disciples saw was a spirit being, not limited by time and space.

   a. John 20:19: Jesus suddenly appeared in a locked room where his disciples were gathered.

   b. Luke 24:15–16: Two of Jesus' followers did not recognize him while they walked together on the road to Emmaus.

3. The resurrection of Jesus Christ restores humanity spiritually but not physically to God.

   a. What the resurrection of Jesus Christ has accomplished

      (1) Jesus' resurrection breaks believers from the Satanic lineage.

      (2) Jesus' resurrection means the return of believers to the heavenly lineage.

      (3) In other words, Christ's resurrection restores the spirit of true believers to God's heavenly dominion.

   b. How to achieve the benefits of Jesus' resurrection

---

[102]*Divine Principle*, 170–71, 360.

[103]Young Oon Kim, *Unification Theology*, 185.

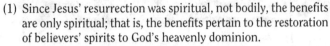

(1) Since Jesus' resurrection was spiritual, not bodily, the benefits are only spiritual; that is, the benefits pertain to the restoration of believers' spirits to God's heavenly dominion.

(2) Believers "come closer" to Jesus' resurrection when they repent of their sins. In other words, repentance begins the process of restoration, but believers must continue to do God's will in order to accomplish the total purpose of Christ's spiritual resurrection; that is, complete restoration to God's heavenly dominion.

(3) As believers daily make themselves better, they come closer to Jesus' resurrection.

c. The limitations of Jesus' resurrection

(1) When Jesus was crucified, Satan invaded his body, thus killing Jesus. (When Moon speaks of "invasion by Satan,"[104] he is not speaking of demon possession, but that the body is still subject to the attacks of Satan upon the flesh. The fallen condition of the flesh was originally caused when Satan physically seduced Eve and whose condition has been passed down to all humans.)

(2) To believe in Jesus means to become one body with Jesus. When Christians become one body with Jesus, "their bodies still remain subject to Satan's invasion," since Satan had invaded Jesus' body.[105]

(3) Therefore, "all the saints since the resurrection of Jesus through the present day have enjoyed the benefits of the providence of spiritual salvation only. Salvation through redemption by the cross is spiritual only."[106]

C. *Refutation of Arguments Used by the Unification Church to Support Its Position on the Resurrection of Jesus Christ*

1. A few people were physically raised from the dead prior to Jesus' bodily resurrection.

a. The Bible offers examples of people who have been physically raised from the dead.

(1) 2 Kings 4:32–35: The prophet Elisha restored the Shunammite boy back to life.

(2) Luke 8:49–55: Jesus raised Jairus's daughter from the dead.

(3) John 11:38–45: Jesus raised Lazarus from the dead after he had been in the tomb for four days.

---

[104]*Divine Principle*, 148.
[105]Ibid.
[106]Ibid.

(4) These examples refute Moon's teaching that the human body cannot be resurrected to its original form after death: Jairus's daughter ate food after coming back to life (Luke 8:55) and the chief priests conspired to kill Lazarus (Luke 12:10).

b. These earlier resurrections were unlike Jesus' resurrection since each went on to die again.

2. After his resurrection, Jesus appeared to his disciples in bodily form.

a. John 20:19

(1) The Bible does not say how Jesus entered the room, just that Jesus suddenly appeared in a closed room where his disciples were gathered (Moon asserts that Jesus entered as a spirit).

(2) Jesus showed his disciples his hands and side, where he had been wounded on the cross (v. 20).

b. Luke 24:16, 31

(1) When Jesus' disciples did not recognize him, the problem was in their ability to perceive. Although Jesus' two followers did not recognize Jesus at first, they realized who he was when he sat at the table with them (v. 31).

(2) They were *prevented* from recognizing Jesus (v. 16). [Note: if Jesus were inherently unrecognizable there would have been no need for God to *prevent* them from recognizing him.]

(3) The issue of recognition cannot be used as an argument against Jesus' physical resurrection.

3. Jesus' resurrection affects both the physical and spiritual attributes of a believer.

a. The Christian's body is a temple of God (1 Cor. 3:16; 6:19).

(1) Paul exhorted the Christians in Corinth not to commit sexual (physical) sins.

(2) If Christ's resurrection lacked the power to affect a believer's physical temptations, why would Paul assume that a Christian could prevail?

(3) Paul wrote to the Christians in Rome that since believers are united with Christ in his resurrection, they are freed from the bondage of sin in their bodies (Rom. 6:5–7).

b. There is a bodily resurrection for those who are in Christ (Rom. 8:11, 23; Phil. 3:20–21).

(1) Christ's resurrection is the firstfruits of believers (1 Cor. 15:20–23); that is, because Jesus was raised from the dead, believers will also be raised from the dead with imperishable bodies (vv. 42, 52).

(2) This is not to say that only Christians will be raised from the dead. All must stand before the Lord's judgment seat (see also

Job 19:26), but only those in Christ will possess an "imperishable body."

4. People cannot *earn* the benefits of Jesus' resurrection.

    a. Although God does require repentance and faithfulness, people cannot merit the benefits that come from Christ's resurrection (Rom. 4:5; 5:9–10; Eph. 2:8–10).

    b. Jesus said he came to save sinners not the righteous (Matt. 9:13).

    c. No one has the ability (Rom. 3:10) or the inclination (v. 12) to do good apart from the power of the Holy Spirit (Rom. 7:18; 8:2; cf. Eph. 2:10).

    d. Jesus said, "Apart from me you can do nothing" (John 15:5).

5. The crucifixion did not limit the power of Jesus' resurrection.

    a. Although Jesus did die on the cross, and in one sense it was a tragic moment, that does not mean that Satan invaded Jesus' body.

    b. If Satan had defeated Jesus on the cross, he would have retained control over Jesus' body by keeping him physically dead and not have allowed Jesus to return to his disciples, who were crushed and hopeless by his death.

    c. Jesus, however, defeated the powers of evil on the cross (Col. 2:15; Heb. 2:14–15).

    d. Since Jesus defeated his enemies, he extended that victory to his followers (1 Cor. 15:54–57), who seeing his resurrected body, were inspired to spread the gospel despite suffering, physical torture, and martyrdom (Acts 5:17–42; 2 Cor. 6:4–10).

D. *Arguments Used to Prove the Biblical Doctrine of the Resurrection of Jesus Christ*

1. Jesus was raised bodily from the dead.

    a. Jesus predicted that his body would be resurrected (John 2:19–22).

        (1) After Jesus drove the money changers out of the temple in Jerusalem, his Jewish critics demanded of him, "What miraculous sign can you show us to prove your authority to do all this?" (v. 18). So Jesus gave them a "sign": "Destroy this temple, and I will raise it again in three days" (v. 19). Jesus' Jewish critics thought he was talking about the temple, "but the temple he had spoken of was his body" (v. 21). After Jesus "was raised from the dead, his disciples recalled what he had said. Then they believed the Scripture and the words that Jesus had spoken" (v. 22).

        (2) Jesus' disciples would not have believed in Jesus unless he was bodily resurrected. Death and the forces of evil would have triumphed in their eyes.

b. Historic documents (the gospels) and eyewitness accounts demonstrate that Jesus rose bodily from the dead.

   (1) When Jesus appeared before his disciples the first time, they were afraid because they thought they were seeing a ghost, but Jesus told them to look at his hands and feet and touch him, saying, "a ghost does not have flesh and bones, as you see I have" (Luke 24:39).

   (2) When they still did not believe, Jesus added a further proof of his physical resurrection: in their presence Jesus ate a piece of broiled fish (v. 42).

   (3) Since Thomas had not been present when Jesus first appeared before the disciples, he declared that he would not believe Jesus had been resurrected unless he saw the nail marks in Jesus' hands and put his fingers where the nails had been (John 20:25). A week later Jesus appeared again and told Thomas to put his finger on his hands and side (v. 27).

c. Peter and Paul taught that Jesus was bodily resurrected.

   (1) Acts 2:31–32: Peter preached that when Christ was resurrected, "he was not abandoned to the grave, nor did his body see decay. God has raised this Jesus to life, and we are all witnesses of the fact."

   (2) Colossians 2:9: Paul wrote to the Colossian Christians that "in Christ all the fullness of the Deity lives [present tense] in bodily form."

   (3) Romans 8:11: Paul also told the Roman Christians that their "mortal bodies" will have life after they are raised from the dead just as the risen Christ has bodily life, showing that Christ was bodily resurrected.

   (4) Philippians 3:21: Paul said Christians' bodies will be transformed to be like Jesus Christ's "glorious body."

2. Faith in the resurrection of Jesus Christ justifies us, not our works.

   a. Romans 4:2–3: God counted Abraham righteous because of his faith, not because of his works. Paul went on to say we also are to place our faith in Jesus Christ, whom God raised from the dead (v. 24).

   b. Romans 10:9: Paul drove this point home when he said, "If you confess with your mouth, 'Jesus is Lord,' and believe in your heart that God raised him from the dead, you will be saved."

3. The resurrection of Jesus Christ liberates us from the power of sin and death.

   a. Romans 6:5: Believers are united with both Christ's death and resurrection. Therefore, since sin's control over our body has been rendered powerless because of Christ's death and resurrection, believers are freed from sin's power or dominion (vv. 6–7).

b. 1 Corinthians 15:20–23: Because Jesus was raised from the dead, we also who belong to him will be raised from the dead.

c. John 11:25–26: Jesus said of the resurrection, "I am the resurrection and the life. He who believes in me will live, even though he dies; and whoever lives and believes in me will never die."

d. Thus death will never triumph over those who believe in Jesus because they will ultimately be raised from the dead as Jesus was.

VI. The Doctrine of Hell and Heaven

A. *The Unification Church's Position on Hell and Heaven Briefly Stated*

1. Hell is a spiritual domain ruled by Satan.

2. Hell is the residence of spirits of people who have rejected God and have died.

3. These people reside in hell until the Lord of the Second Advent has redeemed all humanity and terminated hell.

4. After their redemption, all human beings will ultimately become divine spirits and dwell in heaven with God.

B. *Arguments Used by the Unification Church to Support Its Position on Hell and Heaven*

1. Hell is any place where Satan rules.[107]

a. Earthly hell is every place on earth where people serve Satan and have succumbed to their evil nature.

b. Spiritual hell is where wicked people go after they die.

c. This spiritual world is also under the dominion of Satan.

2. People who have rejected God, Christ, or the Lord of the Second Advent will go to hell after they die.

a. Even those people who believe they are Christians but who reject the Lord of the Second Advent will go to hell.[108]

b. Nevertheless, everyone will inevitably come to believe in the Lord of the Second Advent.

c. People in hell will come to realize the truth about the Lord of the Second Advent, become his followers, and be delivered from hell.

3. Inevitably, God will redeem every human being—past, present, and future.[109]

---

[107]*Divine Principle*, 103.
[108]Ibid., 535.
[109]Ibid., 187–90.

a. Why God will save everyone

   (1) If hell were to remain eternally, hell's existence would contradict the perfect goodness of God.

   (2) Young Oon Kim adds, "[eternal] hell is a pagan idea totally contrary to the Christian faith in a God of immeasurable love."[110]

b. What God will do with evil people and hell

   (1) Even evil people will believe in the Lord of the Second Advent and earn the benefits of God's heavenly kingdom.

   (2) Since everyone will come to believe in the Lord of the Second Advent, they will serve him and become perfect.

   (3) At that time God will abolish hell.

4. Inevitably everyone will become divine.

a. The three ages of redemption[111]

   (1) The Old Testament Age lasted 2000 years, from Abraham to Jesus.[112]

   (2) The New Testament Age also lasted 2000 years, from Jesus to the Lord of the Second Advent.

   (3) The Completed Testament Age will endure forever, beginning with the rule of the Lord of the Second Advent.

   (4) In addition, "in the Completed Testament Age people will be justified not by observing the Mosaic Law or believing in Jesus, but by following and attending the Lord [Moon] of the new world."[113]

b. The three stages through which people will become divine

   (1) People who obeyed the Mosaic Law during the Old Testament Age entered the spirit world as "form spirits" after they physically die.[114]

   Through their deeds on earth, form spirits have *formed* a relationship with God, though they have not perfected themselves. Moon calls the spirit world simply "the invisible world."[115] It is neither hell, where Satan rules, nor heaven, where God rules.

   (2) People who followed the teachings of Jesus Christ during the New Testament Age enter Paradise as "life spirits" after they physically die.[116]

---

[110] Young Oon Kim, *Unification Theology & Christian Thought* (New York: Golden Gate Publishing, 1975), 150.

[111] *Divine Principle*, 233.

[112] Ibid.

[113] Young Oon Kim, *Divine Principle and Its Application* (Washington, D.C.: HSA-UWC, 1968), 93.

[114] *Divine Principle*, 174.

[115] Ibid., 63.

[116] Ibid., 174–75.

Paradise is a part of the spirit world (not hell or heaven), where God's light shines more than where the form spirits reside.[117] Through God's mercy and because of their belief in Christ, life spirits have a closer relationship with God than form spirits, but they still have not attained perfection.

(3) When people serve the Lord of the Second Advent during the Completed Testament Age, they will enter the heavenly kingdom of God as "divine spirits" when they leave their physical bodies.[118]

The heavenly kingdom of God, where God rules, is accessible to people's spirits after the kingdom of heaven is established on earth.[119] The Lord of the Second Advent will establish the kingdom of Heaven on earth, thus making it possible for people on earth and in the spirit world (both in and out of hell) to become perfect and enter God's heavenly kingdom. Jonathan Wells, a Unification theologian, affirms, "According to *Divine Principle*, human beings are supposed to grow to perfection through 'three orderly stages of growth.' During these stages, God's dominion is 'indirect,' leaving individuals to accomplish their own 'portion of responsibility' by their obedience. This is necessary in order for them to become like God."[120]

c. Where people reside after they die

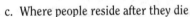

(1) After evil people die, they leave their physical bodies and transmigrate into hell in the spirit world.[121] This hell is a spiritual dominion ruled by Satan, where evil people suffer because of their evil deeds.

(2) After the saints of the Old Testament Age died, they resided in a dark place called a "tomb."[122]

(3) Jesus' resurrection opened up the tomb so that people could enter into Paradise.[123]

(4) Since the time of Jesus' crucifixion, however, no Christian has entered God's heavenly kingdom.[124]

---

[117]Ibid., 117.

[118]Ibid., 175.

[119]Ibid., 62.

[120]*Hermeneutics & Horizons: The Shape of the Future,* ed. Frank K. Flinn (New York: Rose of Sharon Press, 1982), 194.

[121]*Divine Principle,* 103.

[122]Ibid., 117.

[123]Ibid.

[124]Ibid., 176.

(5) Jesus had limited movement in heaven until Heung Jin Nim (Moon's deceased son) empowered Jesus to extend his spiritual capabilities.[125]

d. The way people become divine spirits

(1) People—both past and present—can become perfect and divine spirits only through physical life on earth by serving the Lord of the Second Advent.[126]

(2) People of the spirit world can cooperate with earthly people to accomplish God's will on earth.[127]

On the one hand, the spirit people give earthly people spiritual power and insight to help them achieve the will of God on earth. Spirit people help earthly people through prayers, healings, mighty works, trances, and prophecies.

On the other hand, the spirit people can share the benefit of the godly labors of earthly people to enter higher spiritual stages.

Thus all spirits eventually will become divine spirits when they enter God's heavenly kingdom after the Lord of the Second Advent opens the way for them.

C. Refutation of Arguments Used by the Unification Church to Support Its Position on Hell and Heaven

1. God will not redeem every human being.

a. The existence of hell is consistent with God's perfect goodness.

(1) God's goodness is characterized not only by his love, but also by his justice (Rev. 15:2–4).

(2) Although a judge might feel sad about someone who has been found guilty of a crime, he or she still must sentence that convicted criminal in order for justice to be served (Ps. 9:16–17; Isa. 11:3–4).

(3) Although God wants all people to be saved and come to the knowledge of truth (1 Tim. 2:1–4), his holiness demands that his people be holy and that he separate himself from those who are not holy (Lev. 20:26; Heb. 12:14).

(4) Apart from Christ we are all sentenced to hell for our crimes, which does not mean that God is not good or loving.

(5) Christ suffered the pains of hell in our place according to God's justice (Isa. 53:4–5; Matt. 8:17; 1 Peter 2:23–24). This does not mean a physical descent into a place, but separation

---

[125] Young Whi Kim, one of Moon's earliest followers, claims he received messages from Heung Jin Nim. Young Whi Kim, 185.

[126] *Divine Principle*, 173.

[127] Ibid., 182–84.

from God, which is the essence of hell (see Matt. 27:46; Luke 16:19–26).

b. Not everyone will believe in the Lord of the Second Advent which, according to Unification teaching, is necessary for salvation.

   (1) Even granting the Unification teaching about the Lord of the Second Advent, still not everyone would be saved.

   Not everyone believed in Jesus Christ, who really was the Messiah; even Judas Iscariot, who lived with Jesus for about three years, did not believe in him. Jesus used the parable of the rich man and Lazarus (Luke 16:19–31) to teach that evil people, even when they are told the truth, will not believe. Thus, even if Moon were truly the "Lord of the Second Advent," there would be those who would persist in rejecting the truth. Consequently, since Unificationists teach that belief in the Lord of the Second Advent is necessary for salvation, not everyone will be saved.

   (2) Christians will never believe in the teachings of the *Divine Principle* and Sun Myung Moon's "Lord of the Second Advent."

   Christians believe in the one true Savior, Jesus Christ, as taught by the Bible (John 14:6; Acts 4:12; 1 Tim. 2:5; Heb. 10:8–14). Therefore, true Christians will not accept this "Lord of the Second Advent" teaching, contrary to the Unification belief that all eventually will.

c. God will not abolish hell.

   (1) The Bible describes the punishment of hell as "eternal" punishment, meaning that it will not end (Matt. 25:41, 46; Jude 7; Rev. 14:9–11; 19:1–3; 20:10).

   (2) Some people will not want to be with God, and in fact will not be—that separation in itself is hell (2 Thess. 1:5–9; Rev. 16:8–11).

2. People will not become divine.

   a. The definition of divine[128]

      (1) It is "being or having the nature of a deity."

      (2) It is being "godlike."

      (3) It is being "holy" and "supremely good."

      (4) It is being "heavenly; perfect."

   b. How Christians can assume some divine qualities through Jesus Christ

      (1) 2 Corinthians 5:1: Since God has built an eternal home for them in heaven, Christians will be *immortal*.

---

[128]*The American Heritage Dictionary*, 2d ed. (Boston: Houghton Mifflin, 1982), 412.

      (2) Hebrews 10:14: Jesus' sacrifice has made Christians *perfect* (sinless) while being made *holy*.

  c. No one will become divine in the sense of absolute deity.

      (1) Even believers will not have the divine nature of God, being all-knowing and all-powerful. Although Peter said we will "participate in the divine nature" (2 Peter 1:4), he was referring to the Holy Spirit dwelling in believers.

      (2) We will always be created beings.

      (3) In heaven we will not be divine spirits equal with God, but we will bow down and worship God the Father, Son, and Holy Spirit (Isa. 66:23; Rom. 14:11; Phil. 2:9–11).

      (4) Although Moon teaches that he has surpassed Jesus in spiritual knowledge and power, he has yet to evidence any of Jesus' divine powers, such as miraculously healing the sick, exorcising demons, calming storms, turning water into wine, or raising people from the dead.

      One could argue that the apostles did some of these miraculous things and they are not divine. But if Moon claims to be greater than Jesus, why has he not even come up to the level of the apostles? Jesus claimed to be divine and demonstrated miraculous powers as proof; the apostles made no claims to deity, but demonstrated derived divine powers. Moon makes phenomenal claims about himself, but does not demonstrate miraculous powers.

3. The Bible condemns spiritism.

  a. Although Moon teaches that people in the spirit world are in contact with his followers and are helping them establish the kingdom of heaven on earth, God specifically commanded his people not to engage in such activity.

      (1) Leviticus 19:26, 31: One of God's laws is that his people not practice divination or turn to mediums and spiritists.

      (2) 2 Kings 23:24: King Josiah of Judah got rid of the spiritists to fulfill the requirements of God's law.

  b. The writers of the New Testament also warned believers about the dangers of spiritism.

      (1) 1 Timothy 4:1: In Paul's instructions to Timothy, Paul pointed out that some will abandon the faith and follow deceiving spirits.

      (2) 1 John 4:1–6: John cautioned believers to test the spirits, distinguishing between the Spirit of God and the spirits of the antichrist.

D. Arguments Used to Prove the Biblical Doctrine of Hell and Heaven

1. Everlasting Punishment

   a. Jesus taught that some will dwell with him in heaven and others will be lost forever.

      (1) Matthew 25:1–13: The parable of the ten virgins shows that the five wise virgins will be with the bridegroom (Jesus Christ) and the five foolish virgins will be rejected by him.

      (2) Matthew 25:14–30: The parable of the talents shows that the faithful servant will be rewarded in the master's home (heaven), while the wicked servant will be cast into the darkness of hell.

      (3) Matthew 25:31–46: In his illustration of the sheep and the goats (believers and nonbelievers), Jesus concluded his warning by saying, "Then they will go away to *eternal punishment*, but the righteous to eternal life."

      (4) Mark 9:44: Jesus said it is better to be maimed than "to go into hell, where the fire never goes out."

   b. The apostles and prophets taught that there is eternal punishment.

      (1) Revelation 20:10–15: John said anyone whose name is not in the book of life will be cast into the lake of fire, and they will be tormented forever (see also Exod. 32:33; Ps. 69:28; Dan. 12:1–2; Rev. 21:27).

      (2) 2 Thessalonians 1:8–9: God will punish with everlasting destruction those who do not know him and do not obey the gospel of Jesus Christ.

      (3) Jude 7: Jude said the people of Sodom and Gomorrah serve as an example of those who will "suffer the punishment of eternal fire."

      (4) Isaiah 66:14–16: At the end of Isaiah's prophecy, the Lord declared that those who rebel against him will suffer the eternal fire of hell.

2. Entry into Heaven Through Jesus Christ

   a. Jesus promised eternal life in God's heavenly kingdom for those who follow him.

      (1) Matthew 19:29: After Jesus spoke to the rich man about how to enter the kingdom of God, he promised his disciples that they would inherit eternal life because they had sacrificed all for him.

      (2) John 6:46–47: Jesus also told his Jewish critics that only he had seen God, but that everyone who believed in him would have everlasting life.

  (3) John 14:1–42: Not only will Jesus' followers inherit eternal life, but also they will have a place in heaven. In fact, Jesus said to his disciples that he would prepare a place in heaven for them when he returned to his father after his death, resurrection, and ascension.

 b. The apostles also taught that, because of Christ, believers will have a place in heaven.

  (1) 1 Peter 3:22: Peter wrote that Jesus Christ has gone into heaven and is at God's right hand (which contradicts the *Divine Principle*'s statement that no one has entered heaven where God resides).

  (2) 1 Peter 1:3–4: Peter said that believers in Christ have a new birth kept in heaven through Jesus Christ.

  (3) 2 Corinthians 5:1: Paul also said that believers have an eternal heavenly house built by God.

3. What Heaven Will Be Like

 a. Luke 20:34–35: Jesus said there will be no marriages in heaven, which conflicts with Moon's theological emphasis on physical and spiritual marriages.

 b. Revelation 21:4: In heaven there will be no more death, mourning, or suffering.

 c. Revelation 21:1: In the new heaven (and new earth) all humans and angels will bow down and worship only God (cf. also Isa. 65:17; 66:22–23; 2 Peter 3:13; Rev. 22:9).

Part III:
Witnessing Tips

I. Suggested Approaches to Witnessing to Members of the Unification Church

A. *Treat people as individuals.*

1. People join the Unification Church for a variety of reasons, and it is important to understand the reason why they are in the Unification Church.

2. Christians need to be sensitive to the individual motivations and needs, and approach each Unificationist accordingly.

3. In most cases there is a combination of reasons why people have become members of the Unification Church, and most, if not all, probably need to be addressed.

4. The point is, when it comes to a one-on-one encounter between a Christian and a Unificationist, the Christian should first discover who the Unificationist is before discussing Christianity.

B. *Understand the most common reasons people join the Unification Church.*

1. Some Unificationists are bitter against traditional religion.

   a. Some people become members of the Unification Church because they are bitter from their experiences with traditional religion and view the Unification Church as refreshing and trustworthy.

   b. Stoner and Parke point out that many Unificationists feel that the traditional church "doesn't stand for anything at all."[129] This statement reflects a reaction to the hypocrisy and lack of true faith they previously observed in churches.

   c. Although it might be tempting to point out similar inconsistencies between what the Unification Church teaches and what is actually practiced, this area should be minimized as a topic for discussion.

      (1) In most cases, this approach only makes them feel defensive and judged, which is one of the reasons they left their traditional religion in the first place.

---

[129]Stoner and Parke, 78.

       (2) Many members who have been in the Unification Church for a couple of years or more already struggle with these inconsistencies.

   d. Acknowledge the hypocrisies and shortcomings of the Christian church.

       (1) That way they will realize that you understand their misgivings and do not feel threatened.

       (2) This acknowledgment also diffuses any attempt on their side to link the failings of some Christians to what you really believe.

   e. Focus on how Jesus Christ has changed you as a person.

       (1) Be specific and open.

          If Christ has made you more patient, explain how impatience was a problem with you before, how he made you patient, and what fruits you are bearing as a Christian who is more patient. In short, the more committed you are to Christ, the more effective will be your witness of him.

       (2) Unificationists need to see that Christianity changes lives.

          If they do, this will contradict what the Unification Church has taught them about Christians. This will also conflict with their personal views of Christianity.

2. Some Unificationists are idealistic.

   a. Some people become members of the Unification Church because they are idealistic, and believe the best way to better the world is through the Unification Church.

   b. In Eileen Barker's words: "The potential recruit is likely to have been seeking for self-fulfillment indirectly by seeking a practical way of improving the world."[130]

   c. Many of the people in this category have had little or no upbringing in any religious tradition.

       (1) Although they probably have not had a bad experience with traditional Christianity, they might hold general misconceptions of Christians, fostered by the news and entertainment media, such as the portrayal of all evangelical Christians as bigoted and self-serving.

       (2) The doctrines of the *Divine Principle* certainly support that image of Christians.

   d. If the Unificationist brings up these charges against Christians, these assumptions should be refuted.

       (1) Of course, your response should not be given in anger, and you should acknowledge that these sins do exist within the church.

---

[130]Barker, 227.

    (2) Argue that this characterization of Christians in general is distorted, biased, and simply untrue.

  e. Discuss what Christians are doing locally and globally to help people in need.

    (1) Instead of criticizing the social impact of the Unification Church, describe specific ministries that are addressing specific social problems (for example, how World Vision is working in an Indonesian community to develop an irrigation system for a destitute people).

    (2) The more familiar you are with various Christian ministries, the more you show that both Christians and you have the same concerns to help people in need.

    (3) Avoid talking about how you and your church go to places like convalescent homes.

    To many non-Christians, these types of activities seem like a token gesture of a Christian's faith. Although these ministries are certainly good, they simply are not effective in this type of discussion.

3. Some Unificationists need to be part of a family.

  a. Some people become members of the Unification Church because they feel they are part of a family.

  b. Ronald Enroth quotes a former member as saying, "It was always a parent-child relationship. The people I brought into the group even called me 'mom.' And they were my 'sons' and 'daughters' whom I provided for physically and emotionally."[131]

  c. The Unification Church promotes a family-type intimacy among its members.

    (1) That is why they have called themselves the "Unified Family."

    (2) Both their doctrines and practices emphasize the importance of the family; that is, working together as brothers and sisters in the Unification Church and serving their Father, Sun Myung Moon, and their Mother, Hak Ja Han.

    (3) For those who have not known the love and positive nurturing of a family, the Unification Church meets this deep need that is within all of us.

  d. Refrain from criticizing the character of Sun Myung Moon when talking with this type of Unificationist.

    (1) They probably have already heard all the negative remarks about Moon in the press and perhaps from Christians.

    (2) They have been taught that Moon is a martyr, and such criticism only reinforces this teaching.

---

[131]Enroth, 103.

(3) They have a respect and love for Moon as a parental figure, so attacking Moon personally would be akin to attacking someone's father.

e. Develop a friendship with the "family-oriented" Unificationist.

(1) It does no good to enlighten them with the truth, and then let them be. Many people who leave the Unification Church return because their need for family is stronger than their concern about any theological issues.

(2) What they need is a better relationship with you (and other Christians) than any they have in the Unification Church—a relationship that is characterized by caring, accountability, and freedom.

(3) In other words, the approach to the "family-oriented" Unificationist requires the commitment to develop a good friendship with this person over a long time.

4. Unificationists believe the doctrines they are taught.

a. Some people remain members of the Unification Church primarily because they believe in the doctrines taught in the Unification Church.

b. John T. Biermans, an attorney and member of the Unification Church, says, "Unificationists are motivated by an intense religious faith grounded in a comprehensive set of beliefs."[132]

c. They probably believe Sun Myung Moon is the Lord of the Second Advent.

d. During a theological discussion with these people, it is best not to get sidetracked by peripheral doctrinal issues.

(1) Since Unificationists can either quote Bible verse after Bible verse—particularly those who are theologically trained—or can bring up one doctrinal issue after another, it can be extremely frustrating to try to persuade them that there are any fallacies in the doctrines of the *Divine Principle*.

(2) Such discussions are fine if the purpose is simply to debate theology, but they don't usually bring them closer to a saving relationship with Christ.

(3) Such issues as whether Lucifer physically seduced Eve, or whether John was the cause for the Jews' disbelief in Jesus as the Messiah, can be discussed but they should not become the central focus of the discussion.

e. Discuss who Jesus is and what he accomplished as the Lord and Savior.

---

[132]*The Odyssey of New Religious Movements: A Case Study of the Unification Church* (Lewiston, N.Y.: Edwin Mellen, 1986), 169.

(1) Discuss central (not peripheral) points of theology (refer to Part II).

(2) It does not matter if you convince them that Moon's theology is heretical but do not persuade them to accept Jesus Christ as their Lord and Savior.

(3) How well you know what the Bible says about Christ will greatly affect your discussion on Jesus Christ.

5. Some Unificationists are looking for an authority figure.

   a. Some people become members of the Unification Church because they want to be under an authority figure, and Sun Myung Moon fulfills that need.

   b. Moon is a charismatic leader with an awe-inspiring and winsome personality.

     (1) Ruth Tucker observes that, "as a superhuman religious figure, Moon has been enveloped in fantasy and myth" by his followers.[133]

     (2) For example, his followers claim that, "Whenever he went to the zoo, all the animals would run over to that part of the zoo. When he visited a fish pond, all the fish would swim over to him."[134]

   c. These people do not seek to become robots under Moon's control, but they want someone they can trust to give them spiritual and moral guidance.

     (1) Because the news and entertainment media in our society constantly attack traditional authority figures—parents, police, teachers, ministers—many people are searching for someone or something to fill that void.

     (2) Not only does Sun Myung Moon demand respect and submission to his will, but the church also instructs followers in every area of their lives.

     (3) They allow Moon and the church to make important decisions on their behalf—including whom they will marry.

   d. Again, it is not helpful to attack the character of Sun Myung Moon.

     (1) Unless you are Asian, and in some cases Korean, they will perceive your criticism as racism.

     (2) Attacking practices within the Unification Church that our society ridicules and that pertain directly to Moon's role as leader is also questionable.

---

[133]Tucker, 246.
[134]Enroth, 108.

For example, the press and people in the United States ridicule the wedding ceremonies, which Moon conducts worldwide, because he has paired the couples and because so many are married at once. In the Unification Church, this ceremony is a sacrament that symbolizes the extent to which the participants have achieved redemption. Also, the selection of spouses by a third party, as well as other practices, are not strange customs in other cultures. Thus Western critics are viewed as provincial and narrow-minded.

   e. Focus on the character of Jesus Christ, especially his leadership qualities.

      (1) Agree with them that many people in our society lack a healthy respect for society and need to respect the authorities that God puts in our lives.

      (2) Explain why Christ is the most important authority figure in your life, how you submit to him, and how he has cared for you.

      (3) Through the power of the Holy Spirit, they may comprehend the vast difference between Jesus Christ and Sun Myung Moon as authority figures.

      (4) How clearly they view Christ in what you share with them is largely determined by how committed you are to Christ.

6. There are other reasons people join the Unification Church besides those listed above.

   a. Although the reasons listed are the most common, they do not account for every case.

   b. Some like the political agenda of the church. Others feel the church has encouraged and supported an artistic or athletic gift that they have which would have gone unrecognized. Still others believe the Unification Church values their individual worth by giving them special tasks.

C. *Know what to focus on to reach the Unification Church member.*

   1. Always make Christ the central focus of your discussion.

      a. You can be a terrific friend to a Unificationist, but if you never speak about Jesus Christ, you are neglecting to share the best friend he or she can have.

      b. Remember that most Unificationists hold Jesus in high regard.

         (1) Unificationists already believe that Jesus was a profound teacher and an ideal servant of God.

         (2) What you should emphasize is that only through Jesus Christ can a person overcome sin and have peace with God.

   2. Be sensitive to the guidance of the Holy Spirit.

The Holy Spirit will give you God's love, patience, kindness, gentleness, self-control, and other qualities that will help you discern what to say and when to say it.

3. Pray for discernment while interacting with people in the Unification Church.

a. Paul told the Christians in Thessalonica to pray continually (1 Thess. 5:17).

(1) Paul's instruction is good advice for Christians in all circumstances.

(2) Christians should remember to follow Paul's advice whenever they are making a defense for the gospel.

b. Pray before, during, and after meeting with a member of the Unification Church.

(1) Before the meeting, ask God to put you in the right frame of mind for the meeting and to prepare the person's heart and mind for the good news about Jesus Christ.

This is especially important when dealing with Unificationists because, as members of the Unification Church, they are deeply involved with spirit contact.

(2) During the meeting, ask God to help you discern what the person needs to hear and recall what you know about Christ—especially applicable Scriptures.

(3) Share the gospel in pairs. Jesus sent out his disciples in twos (Mark 6:7; Luke 10:1). This strategy has practical value as well: while one person is explaining the gospel, the other can pray that the Holy Spirit will remove the veil of Moon's false teachings.

(4) After the meeting, ask God what other ways you can help this person know Christ, and pray that this person will receive Jesus Christ as his or her Lord and Savior.

Keep praying for your Unificationist friend. More than once I have seen Unificationists come to Christ, even though they seemed firmly committed to the Unification Church.

4. Study the Bible regularly to be ready to effectively share the gospel with people in the Unification Church.

a. Kenneth Boa, veteran researcher of the cults, believes, "cults like Moon's, which purport to be based in part on the Bible, should remind us of our need to know the teachings of Scripture."[135]

b. Paul told Timothy to be prepared in season and out of season to preach the Word (2 Tim. 4:2).

---

[135]Kenneth Boa, *Cults, World Religions and the Occult* (Wheaton, Ill.: Victor, 1992), 222.

    (1) That means Christians should study what the Bible teaches about Jesus Christ so that they will be ready whenever they are called upon to share the gospel.

    (2) When Christians meet people who belong to the Unification Church, they should be able to turn to key Scriptures to support their belief about Christ.

    (3) If a Christian sets up a Bible study with a Unificationist, he or she should be familiar with key books of the Bible that teach on the person and work of Jesus Christ.

  c. Certain biblical passages are particularly helpful when sharing the gospel with people in the Unification Church.

    (1) Concerning the deity of Christ: the Gospel of John and Colossians.

    (2) Concerning Christ's atonement on the cross: Paul's letters to the Romans (the first eight chapters) and Galatians, and particularly the Letter to the Hebrews.

    (3) Concerning Christ's resurrection: Luke 24.

5. Be prepared to ask the right questions.

  a. What to ask Unificationists about Christ

    (1) Most members of the Unification Church have a high regard for Jesus Christ, and they sincerely believe they are Christians, though not like other Christians.

    (2) They do not believe Jesus was a failure, but that people failed him.

    (3) If they have any aversions, they are to traditional Christians and the traditional Christian church, not to Christ.

    (4) At the same time they will want to find common ground with Christians, to form some kind of Christian fellowship and avoid the crucial differences in our beliefs.

    (5) Therefore, you should not approach them with the idea of attacking how they feel about Christ, but rather to establish exactly what they believe Jesus has accomplished on the cross.

    (6) Once you begin to share the gospel with a Unificationist, the question you want to ask is, "Do you believe Jesus Christ has completely cleansed us of all our sins once and for all time when he died on the cross?" Then ask them why.

  b. What to ask Unificationists about Moon

    (1) It has already been suggested not to attack Moon's character, but rather point out how his theology conflicts with biblical teaching.

    (2) Do not ask them whether they believe Moon is the Messiah.

    First, most of them do not want to argue about this issue, believing people will come to accept Moon after they see the good things about his church first. Second, even if they do believe Moon is the Messiah, they can say he is a man of God, a prophet, or a great teacher, but claim they do not know whether he is the Messiah. They can say this without the pretense of lying, on the grounds that Moon has not accomplished everything the Lord of the Second Advent must do to fulfill God's plan of redemption. They believe, however, that Moon will ultimately accomplish all those things.

(3) Instead, when contrasting Moon with Christ, the question to ask is, "Will you deny that Sun Myung Moon is the Messiah?"

Although it might seem as though this question allows them to hedge like the other question, it usually forces them to concede more of what they believe than they otherwise would have. After you insist that they answer your question with a yes or no (which you could not do with the other question), ask them why they cannot make this denial.

c. After you have solicited answers to these two questions, the people may be ready to receive the gospel—if their hearts are willing to hear the good news about Jesus Christ.

II. Approaches to Avoid in Witnessing to Members of the Unification Church

A. False Assumptions

1. Why Unificationists Are Stereotyped

   a. Because of the bizarre, and sometimes violent, behavior of some cultists, people sometimes think that all unorthodox religious groups are the same.

   b. The news and entertainment media usually focus on the sensational and then make generalized statements, such as comparing Sun Myung Moon with Jim Jones and David Koresh, thereby conveying false impressions of a leader and his group.

   c. Christian authors who are not experts about a specific group but who write about an array of cults, often lack firsthand knowledge about the group, and therefore make false generalizations. Unfortunately, many are best-selling authors whose statements become widely accepted.

2. False Assumptions About People in the Unification Church

   a. Many people believe the Unification Church has brainwashed its members.

      (1) It is true that questionable practices have occurred within the Unification Church (as mentioned in Part I).

    (2) Whether national leaders have encouraged the systematic use of psychological techniques or local leaders used them on their own initiative is no longer relevant, since recruiting practices have been modified to avert continued censure.

    (3) Regardless of the reasons why people join the Unification Church, members seem to remain in the church on their own volition.

    In fact, I know of cases in which authorities in the Unification Church sent members home to their families because they felt these people could not function as effective members within their church. In addition, sociologists Thomas Robbins and Dick Anthony found that many people left the Unification Church easily and voluntarily.[136]

  b. Some people think that Unificationists are capable of violence and mass suicide.

    (1) Some political and evangelistic statements of Moon have been taken out of context and used to foster this impression of this group.

    (2) The extraordinary devotion to Moon and his movement by most Unificationists lead people to compare them with extremist groups.

    (3) Most of the people in the highest levels of the Unification Church, however, are too academically inclined and business-minded to allow their church to dissolve in this way.

  c. Many people assume that most Unificationists cannot function normally in society, and that is why they are in this group.

    (1) While this statement is probably true for some of its members, all groups—religious and non-religious—have some dysfunctional people.

    (2) Many Unification members are articulate, content, and quite normal.

    (3) It would be a mistake to assume that all Unificationists are maladjusted.

B. Unhelpful Behaviors

  1. As was mentioned earlier, avoid attacking the character of Sun Myung Moon.

    a. When a Christian is trying to share the gospel with a Unificationist, attacking Moon's character will only harden the person's heart.

    b. At the same time, Christians should challenge Moon's theology.

---

[136]Robbins and Anthony, 264–65.

    c. Of course, when one Christian who is knowledgeable about Moon and his movement is informing other Christians about this group, he or she can address the character of Moon.

2. Refrain from calling them "Moonies."

    a. Refer to them as Unificationists.

    b. Although they may not express displeasure when you refer to them as "Moonies," for many it is a derogatory term.

    c. Christians are often guilty of this, not because they intend to insult them, but because it is a popular and recognizable word.

3. Resist the temptation to be too accommodating to Unificationists, no matter how agreeable and nice they are toward you.

    a. In an effort to be loving, some Christians make unwise decisions in dealing with Unificationists.

       (1) You might invite them to join your church Bible study group, which can disturb the dynamics and primary purpose of the group.

       (2) You might go alone to one of their weekend retreats without any Christian training on how to deal with Unificationists in their settings.

       (3) You might identify yourself with one of their political or social causes because you agree with some of their points.

    b. Jesus' statement is quite appropriate: "Be as shrewd as snakes and as innocent as doves" (Matt. 10:16).

Part IV:
Selected Bibliography

I. Works Published by the Unification Church

A. *The Works of Sun Myung Moon*

America in God's Providence. New York: Unification Church of America, 1976.

Christianity in Crisis. Washington, D.C.: The Holy Spirit Association for the Unification of World Christianity, 1974.

Divine Principle. 2d ed. Washington, D.C.: The Holy Spirit Association for the Unification of World Christianity, 1973.

The *Divine Principle* is the authoritative document of the Unification Church. Although other books provide spiritual guidance to Unificationists, the *Divine Principle* is the only book that nearly all Unificationists accept.

Master Speaks

This is a collection of Moon's sermons to his followers. Because Moon preaches in Korean, these sermons are translated into English, which allows Unification spokespersons to say that some of his quotes sound notorious because of translation problems. Nevertheless, these sermons provide further explanations of Moon's teaching, continuing on points where the *Divine Principle* leaves off. These sermons are circulated among members, who honor all that Moon teaches.

New Hope: Twelve Talks. 2 vols. New York: The Holy Spirit Association for the Unification of World Christianity, 1984.

B. *The Works of Young Oon Kim*

Divine Principle and Its Application. Washington, D.C.: The Holy Spirit Association for the Unification of World Christianity, 1968.

Young Oon Kim came to the United States in 1959 as a Unification missionary. This book was published in English during the early years of Moon's movement in North America. It was used to explain many of the more difficult passages of the *Divine Principle*.

Unification Theology. New York: The Holy Spirit Association for the Unification of World Christianity, 1980.

This book is an updated, extensive revision of Young Oon Kim's previous book. Although the theological sophistication of the Unification Church (in many ways) has advanced beyond this book, it is still useful in understanding Moon's doctrine on the spirit world and spirit beings.

Unification Church Training Manuals

Unification officials use training manuals to educate potential leaders and apologists. These manuals contain lectures and presentations from training sessions. They offer personal experiences of practical ways to apply *Divine Principle* teachings. The material also reveals their attitude toward non-Unificationists, especially Christians.

Unification Church Newsletters

The Unification Church distributes newsletters, such as the "New Hope News," and a vast amount of other literature within its church and affiliate groups. At times these materials are informative about the history of their church, current news and changes within their church, and immediate goals of their church. Taken together, Unification literature indicates how broad is the outreach of Moon's movement both socially and economically.

II. Works Written About the Unification Church by Nonmembers

A. Literature Sympathetic to the Unification Church

Quebedeaux, Richard. *Lifestyle: Conversations with Members of the Unification Church*. Barrytown, N.Y.: Unification Theological Seminary, 1982.

Quebedeaux is best known for his book, *The Worldly Evangelicals*, in which he points out how many evangelicals have adopted worldly values. Although Quebedeaux is not a member of the Unification Church and has reservations about their theology, he praises the dedication of the Unificationists, and has taught regularly at the Unification Theological Seminary in Barrytown, New York.

Quebedeaux, Richard, and Ordney Sawatsky, eds. *Evangelical-Unification Dialogue*. New York: Rose of Sharon Press, 1979.

Leading evangelical critics of the Unification Church met with theologians of the Unification Church to discuss Christology and other Christian doctrines. (I participated in these conferences.) These discussions revealed interesting internal theological differences within the Unification Church. For example, some Unificationist theologians expressed a deep reverance for Jesus while others had little respect for him.

Sherwood, Carlton. *Inquisition: The Persecution and Prosecution of the Reverend Sun Myung Moon*. Washington, D.C.: Regnery Gateway, 1991.

Sherwood is a veteran journalist who has won the Pulitzer Prize for investigative reporting of religious corruption. Although his book is quite biased in favor of Moon and his church, it provides a fascinating account of Moon's indictment, prosecution, conviction, and sentencing for tax evasion, asking disturbing questions about how and why the judicial system handled Moon's case.

Sontag, Frederick. *Sun Myung Moon and the Unification Church*. Nashville: Abingdon, 1977.

A respected scholar, Sontag approaches the Unification Church from a liberal Christian perspective. His book was the first major non-Unification treatment of Moon that was generally positive about the movement and critical of Moon's detractors. The Unification Church allowed Sontag to interview members and officials of their church, including Moon, and these conversations are included in the book.

B. Personal Accounts from Former Unification Church Members

Edwards, Christopher. *Crazy for God: The Nightmare of Cult Life*. Englewood Cliffs, N.J.: Prentice Hall, 1979.

A Yale graduate in psychology, Edwards details his seven months in the Unification Church and how he was reportedly "deprogrammed" (convinced that he was brainwashed and thus renounces the group he was involved with). His account describes the early psychological abuses within the Unification Church. It is written for a secular audience.

Elkins, Chris. *Heavenly Deception*. Wheaton, Ill.: Tyndale House, 1980.

Elkins describes the spiritual deception of Moon and his teachings. He also relates how he became a Christian from his experience.

Elkins, Chris. *What Do You Say to a Moonie?* Wheaton, Ill.: Tyndale House, 1980.

Elkins offers valuable suggestions on how to share the gospel with Unificationists.

Kemperman, Steve. *Lord of the Second Advent*. Ventura, Calif.: Regal Books, 1981.

Kemperman provides insights into the internal activities of the Unification Church.

C. Major Secular Critiques of the Unification Church

Barker, Eileen. *The Making of a Moonie: Choice or Brainwashing?* New York: Basil Blackwell, 1984.

A college professor in England, Barker offers a more up-to-date presentation than what is normally available on library shelves. She is more sympathetic to this movement than previous secular critiques and is inclined to think Christian critics are alarmists, but her book contains valuable information and insight on how Moon's group is evolving from a cult to an established religion.

Bromley, David G., and Anson D. Shupe, Jr. *"Moonies" in America: Cult, Church, and Crusade*. Beverly Hills: Sage Publications, 1979.

These scholars examine the sociological effects of Moon's movement on American society and American Unification members. This was the most important secular treatment of the Unification Church in the 70s and early 80s because of its fine academic research.

77

Stoner, Carroll, and Jo Anne Parke. *All God's Children: The Cult Experience—Salvation or Slavery?* Radnor, Penn.: Chilton Book Company, 1977.

These professional reporters examine the activities of cults in the United States during the late 60s and early 70s from a journalistic perspective. Their book received national attention and helped form the early public image of Moon and his church.

D. *Major Christian Critiques of the Unification Church*

Bjornstad, James. *Sun Myung Moon and the Unification Church.* Minneapolis: Bethany House, 1984.

This book is an updated version of his earlier treatment of the Unification Church, *The Moon Is Not the Son.* This is a good, general survey of Moon's movement.

Enroth, Ronald. "Unification Church." Chap. 10 in *A Guide to Cults & New Religions.* Downers Grove, Ill.: InterVarsity Press, 1983.

This chapter examines Unification history and doctrines while providing a Christian critique.

Enroth, Ronald. "The Unification Church." Chap. 5 in *Youth, Brainwashing and the Extremist Cults.* Grand Rapids: Zondervan, 1977.

This chapter contains a case study of a young Jewish woman who became a Unificationist and then was "deprogrammed." Enroth argues that people in cults should be deprogrammed because he believes many are brainwashed.

Martin, Walter. "Unification Church." Chap. 13 in *The Kingdom of the Cults.* Rev. and exp. edition. Minneapolis: Bethany House, 1985.

This chapter includes background on Moon and his church with some biblical critique of Moon's doctrines. This Christian classic on the cults is the most readily available book on the Unification Church.

Tucker, Ruth A. "The Unification Church: Proclaiming a New Messiah." Chap. 11 in *Another Gospel: Alternative Religions and the New Age Movement.* Grand Rapids: Zondervan, 1989.

In addition to cursory examination of Moon's theology and church history, Tucker provides information about events pertaining to Moon's life that are more up-to-date than most other Christian books.

Yamamoto, J. Isamu. *The Puppet Master: An Inquiry into Sun Myung Moon and the Unification Church.* Downers Grove, Ill.: InterVarsity Press, 1977.

This comprehensive treatment of the Unification Church provides the most serious discussion of the conflict between Moon's theology and the doctrines of orthodox Christianity. This book, however, surveys the history of Moon's church only up to the late 1970s.

Part V:
Parallel Comparison Chart

Unification Church	The Bible

Divine Revelation

"With the fullness of time, God has sent His messenger to resolve the fundamental questions of life and the universe. His name is Sun Myung Moon.... We have recorded here [in the *Divine Principle*] what Sun Myung Moon's disciples have hitherto heard and witnessed" (*Divine Principle*, 16).

"See to it that no one takes you captive through hollow and deceptive philosophy, which depends on human tradition and the basic principles of this world rather than on Christ" (Col. 2:8).

"God revealed to Reverend Moon the fundamental core of his teaching" (Young Oon Kim, *Unification Theology*, 50).

"If anyone teaches false doctrines and does not agree to the sound instruction of our Lord Jesus Christ and to godly teaching, he is conceited and understands nothing" (1 Tim. 6:3–4).

"It may be displeasing to religious believers, especially to Christians, to learn that a new expression of truth must appear. They believe that the Bible, which they now have, is perfect and absolute in itself. Truth, of course, is unique, eternal, unchangeable, and absolute. The Bible, however, is not the truth itself, but a textbook teaching the truth" (*Divine Principle*, 9).

"All Scripture is God-breathed" (2 Tim. 3:16).

"Your word is truth" (John 17:17).

Divine Revelation (cont.)

"Christians of today, who are captives to scriptural words, will surely criticize the words and conduct of the Lord of the Second Advent [Sun Myung Moon], according to the limits of what the New Testament words literally state.... Innumerable Christians of today are dashing on the way which they think will lead them to the Kingdom of Heaven. Nevertheless, this very road is apt to lead them to Hell" (*Divine Principle*, 533, 535).

"Dear friends, do not believe every spirit, but test the spirits to see whether they are from God, because many false prophets have gone out into the world" (1 John 4:1).

Sin

"Many Christians to this day believe that the fruit which caused Adam and Eve to fall was literally the fruit of a tree.... According to what has been elucidated by the Bible, we have come to understand that the root of sin is not that the first human ancestors ate a fruit, but that they had an illicit blood relationship with an angel symbolized by a serpent" (*Divine Principle*, 66, 75).

"When the woman saw that the fruit of the tree was good for food and pleasing to the eye, and also desirable for gaining wisdom, she took some and ate it. She also gave some to her husband, who was with her, and he ate it" (Gen. 3:6).

"The root of man's sin stems from adultery.... Every religion which teaches how to eliminate sin has called adultery the greatest sin.... This also demonstrates that the root of sin lies in adultery" (*Divine Principle*, 75).

"For whoever keeps the whole law and yet stumbles at just one point is guilty of breaking all of it. For he who said, 'Do not commit adultery,' also said, 'Do not murder.' If you do not commit adultery but do commit murder, you have become a lawbreaker" (James 2:10–11).

Sin (cont.)

"Men, without exception, are inclined to repel evil and to pursue goodness" (*Divine Principle*, 65).

"There is no one righteous, not even one; there is no one who understands, no one who seeks God. All have turned away, they have together become worthless; there is no one who does good, not even one" (Rom. 3:10–12; see also Pss. 14:1–3; 53:1–3; Eccl. 7:20).

"Father [Moon] is sinless, Mother [Moon's wife] is sinless, and their children are sinless" (Ken Sudo, "Christology," from *The 120–Day Training Manual*, 236).

"There is no one who does not sin" (1 Kings 8:46).

"If we claim to be without sin, we deceive ourselves and the truth is not in us. . . . If we claim we have not sinned, we make him out to be a liar and his word has no place in our lives" (1 John 1:8, 10).

Salvation

"From the time of Jesus through the present, all Christians have thought that Jesus came to the world to die. This is because they did not know the fundamental purpose of Jesus' coming as the Messiah, and entertained the wrong idea that spiritual salvation was the only mission for which Jesus came to the world. . . . Jesus did not come to die" (*Divine Principle*, 152).

"How foolish you are, and how slow of heart to believe all that the prophets have spoken! Did not the Christ have to suffer these things and then enter his glory?" (Luke 24:25–26).

"This man was handed over to you by God's set purpose and foreknowledge; and you, with the help of wicked men, put him to death by nailing him to the cross" (Acts 2:23).

"Jesus was then resolved to take the cross as the condition of indemnity to pay for the accomplishment of even the spiritual salvation of man when he found that he was unable to accomplish the providence of both spiritual and physical salvation" (*Divine Principle*, 151).

"The blood of Jesus, his [God's] Son, purifies us from all sin" (1 John 1:7).

Salvation (cont.)

"The original self will be restored by removing man's original sin through the Second Advent of the Lord.... We know that now is truly the time for Christ to come again" (*Divine Principle*, 180, 498–99).

"Who could be the male child who is born of a woman with the qualification of sitting on the throne of God, and who will rule all the nations with the words of God? This can be none other than the Lord of the Second Advent who is to be born on the earth as the King of Kings, and who will realize the Kingdom of God on earth.... [He] must come again in order to complete the physical salvation" (*Divine Principle*, 509, 512).

"Therefore, the Lord of the Second Advent must come to restore the whole of mankind to be children of God's direct lineage" (*Divine Principle*, 369).

"Rev. Moon is the Messiah, the Lord of the Second Advent" (Ken Sudo, "Family Problems," from *The 120–Day Training Manual*, 160).

"We atone for our sins through specific acts of penance" (Young Oon Kim, *Unification Theology*, 230).

"Man's perfection must be accomplished finally by his own effort without God's help" (Kwang-Yol Yoo, *New Hope News* [October 7, 1974], 7).

"Christ was sacrificed once to take away the sins of many people; and he will appear a second time, not to bear sin, but to bring salvation to those who are waiting for him" (Heb. 9:28).

"It is by the name of Jesus Christ of Nazareth, whom you crucified but whom God raised from the dead, that this man stands before you healed.... Salvation is found in no one else, for there is no other name under heaven given to men by which we must be saved" (Acts 4:10, 12).

"Yet to all who received him, to those who believed in his [Jesus'] name, he gave the right to become children of God" (John 1:12).

"Jesus answered, 'I am the way and the truth and the life. No one comes to the Father except through me'" (John 14:6).

"For it is by grace you have been saved, through faith—and this not from yourselves, it is the gift of God—not by works, so that no one can boast" (Eph. 2:8–9).

The Deity of Jesus Christ and the Trinity

"However great [Jesus'] value may be, he cannot assume a value greater than that of a man who has attained the purpose of creation" (*Divine Principle*, 209).

"Jesus, from his outward appearance, was no different from ordinary, fallen men" (*Divine Principle*, 171).

"Jesus, on earth, was a man no different from us except for the fact that he was without original sin. Even in the spirit world after his resurrection, he lives as a spirit man with his disciples.... Jesus is not God Himself" (*Divine Principle*, 212).

"Jesus himself says that Heung Jin Nim [Moon's deceased son] is the new Christ [heavenly Messiah]. He is the center of the spirit world now. This means he is in a higher position than Jesus" (Young Whi Kim, *Guidance for Heavenly Tradition* vol. 2, 183).

"Christ [the Lord of the Second Advent] must come again in flesh in order that he may become the True Parent both spiritually and physically, by forming the substantial Trinity centered on God" (*Divine Principle*, 218).

"He [Jesus] is the image of the invisible God, the firstborn over all creation. For by him all things were created: things in heaven and on earth, visible and invisible, whether thrones or powers or rulers or authorities; all things were created by him" (Col. 1:15–16).

"For in Christ all the fullness of the Deity lives in bodily form" (Col. 2:9).

"I [Jesus] and the Father are one" (John 10:30).

"To those who through the righteousness of our God and Savior Jesus Christ have received a faith as precious as ours" (2 Peter 1:1).

"In the beginning was the Word, and the Word was with God and the Word [Jesus] was God. ...The Word became flesh and made his dwelling among us" (John 1:1, 14).

"God exalted him [Jesus] to the highest place and gave him the name that is above every name, that at the name of Jesus every knee should bow, in heaven and on earth and under the earth, and every tongue confess that Jesus Christ is Lord" (Phil. 2:9–11).

"Go and make disciples of all nations, baptizing them in the name of the Father and of the Son and of the Holy Spirit" (Matt. 28:19).

"May the grace of the Lord Jesus Christ, and the love of God, and the fellowship of the Holy Spirit be with you all" (2 Cor. 13:14).

83

The Resurrection of Jesus Christ

"Because the Jewish people disbelieved Jesus and delivered him up for crucifixion, his body was invaded by Satan, and he was killed. Therefore, even when Christians believe in and become one body with Jesus, whose body was invaded by Satan, their bodies still remain subject to Satan's invasion" (*Divine Principle,* 147–48).

"As we know through the Bible, Jesus after the resurrection was not the same Jesus who had lived with his disciples before his crucifixion. He was no longer a man seen through physical eyes, because he was a being transcendent of time and space" (*Divine Principle*, 360).

"The physical resurrection and bodily ascension of Jesus ... are not an essential part of ... faith in Jesus as the risen Lord" (Young Oon Kim, *Unification Theology*, 185).

"Having disarmed the powers and authorities, he [Jesus] made a public spectacle of them, triumphing over them by the cross" (Col. 2:15).

"They [Jesus' disciples] were startled and frightened, thinking they saw a ghost. He said to them, 'Why are you troubled, and why do doubts rise in your minds? Look at my hands and my feet. It is I myself! Touch me and see; a ghost does not have flesh and bones, as you see I have.' When he had said this, he showed them his hands and feet. And while they still did not believe it because of joy and amazement, he asked them, 'Do you have anything here to eat?' They gave him a piece of broiled fish, and he took it and ate it in their presence" (Luke 24:37–43).

"The Jews demanded of him [Jesus], 'What miraculous sign can you show us to prove your authority to do all this?' Jesus answered them, 'Destroy this temple, and I will raise it again in three days.' The Jews replied, 'It has taken forty-six years to build this temple, and you are going to raise it in three days?' But the temple he had spoken of was his body. After he was raised from the dead, his disciples recalled what he had said. Then they believed the Scripture and the words that Jesus had spoken" (John 2:18–22).

Hell and Heaven

"Hell is a pagan idea totally contrary to the Christian faith in a God of immeasurable love" (Young Oon Kim, *Unification Theology & Christian Thought*, 185).

"He [the Lord Jesus] will punish those who do not know God and do not obey the gospel of our Lord Jesus. They will be punished with everlasting destruction and shut out from the presence of the Lord" (2 Thess. 1:8–9).

"Through their works, evil spirit men also are allowed to enter the sphere of benefit of the new age, with the same benefits as earthly men.... The ultimate purpose of God's providence of restoration is to save all mankind. Therefore, it is God's intention to abolish Hell completely" (*Divine Principle*, 187, 190).

"Then they [the wicked] will go away to *eternal punishment*, but the righteous to eternal life" (Matt. 25:46, emphasis added).

"Christians, up to the present, have been confused in their concepts of Heaven and Paradise because they have not known the Principle. If Jesus had accomplished the purpose of his coming on earth as the Messiah, the Kingdom of Heaven on earth would have been established at that time.... The Kingdom of Heaven on earth has not been realized due to the crucifixion of Jesus, and not a single person on earth has attained the divine-spirit stage. Consequently, no spirit man has entered the Heavenly Kingdom of God. . . . Therefore, the Heavenly Kingdom of God still remains vacant" (*Divine Principle*, 176).

"Do not let your hearts be troubled. Trust in God; trust also in me. In my Father's house are many rooms; if it were not so, I would have told you. I am going there to prepare a place for you. And if I go and prepare a place for you, I will come back and take you to be with me that you also may be where I am going" (John 14:1–3).